The Economist

STYLE GUIDE

NEW EDITION

THE ECONOMIST IN ASSOCIATION WITH
HAMISH HAMILTON LTD

Published by the Penguin Group
Penguin Books Ltd, 27 Wrights Lane, London W8 5TZ, England
Penguin Books USA Inc., 375 Hudson Street, New York, New York 10014, USA
Penguin Books Australia Ltd, Ringwood, Victoria, Australia
Penguin Books Canada Ltd, 10 Alcorn Avenue, Toronto, Ontario, Canada M4V 3B2
Penguin Books (NZ) Ltd, 182–190 Wairau Road, Auckland 10, New Zealand

Penguin Books Ltd, Registered Offices: Harmondsworth, Middlesex, England

First published as *The Economist Pocket Style Book* by The Economist Books Ltd 1986
Second edition published under the title *The Economist Style Guide*
by The Economist Books Ltd 1991
Third edition published by Hamish Hamilton in association with
The Economist Books 1993

This edition published by Hamish Hamilton in association with
The Economist Books 1996

10 9 8 7 6 5 4 3 2 1

Copyright © The Economist Books Ltd, 1986, 1991, 1993, 1996

Any correspondence regarding this publication should be addressed to:
The Editorial Director, The Economist Books, 25 St James's Street,
London SW1 1HG

Filmset in

Printed in Great Britain by Clays Ltd, St Ives plc

A CIP catalogue record for this book is available from the British Library

ISBN 0-241-13556-7

CONTENTS

PREFACE   4

INTRODUCTION   5

A NOTE ON EDITING   8

PART I   The Essence of Style   9

PART II   American and British English   73

PART III   Fact Checker and Glossary   87

INDEX   141

PREFACE

Every newspaper has its own style book, a set of rules telling journalists whether to write Peking or Beijing, Gadaffi or Qaddafi, judgement or judgment. *The Economist*'s style book does this and a bit more. It also warns writers of some common mistakes and encourages them to write with more clarity and simplicity.

To make the style guide of wider general interest, additional material has been added, drawing on the series of reference books published under The Economist Books imprint.

All the prescriptive judgments in this style guide, however, are directly derived from those used each week in writing and editing *The Economist*.

Throughout the text, bold type is used to indicate examples. Words in SMALL CAPITALS indicate a separate but relevant entry (except in the paragraphs headed ABBREVIATIONS, where the use of small capitals is discussed).

This new edition of *The Economist Style Guide* is in three sections. The first is based on the style book used by those who edit *The Economist*; it is largely the work of John Grimond, the foreign editor. The second, on American and British English, describes the main differences between the two great English-speaking areas, in spelling, grammar and usage. The third part gathers together in one place lots of useful reference material.

INTRODUCTION

On only two scores can *The Economist* hope to outdo its rivals consistently. One is the quality of its analysis; the other is the quality of its writing. The aim of this style guide is to give general advice on writing, to point out some common errors and to set some arbitrary rules. The first requirement of *The Economist* is that it should be readily understandable. Clarity of writing usually follows clarity of thought. So think what you want to say, then say it as simply as possible. Keep in mind George Orwell's six elementary rules ("Politics and the English Language", 1946):

1. Never use a METAPHOR, simile or other figure of speech which you are used to seeing in print.
2. Never use a long word where a SHORT WORD will do.
3. If it is possible to cut out a word, always cut it out.
4. Never use the passive where you can use the ACTIVE.
5. Never use a FOREIGN PHRASE, a scientific word or a JARGON word. if you can think of an everyday English equivalent.
6. Break any of these rules sooner than say anything outright barbarous.

Readers are primarily interested in what you have to say. By the way in which you say it you may encourage them either to read on or to stop reading. If you want them to read on:

1. Do not be stuffy. "To write a genuine, familiar or truly English style", said Hazlitt, "is to write as anyone would speak in common conversation who had a thorough command or choice of words or who could discourse with ease, force and perspicuity setting aside all pedantic and oratorical flourishes."

Use the language of everyday speech, not that of spokesmen, lawyers or bureaucrats (so prefer **let** to **permit**, **people** to **persons**, **buy** to **purchase**, **colleague** to **peer**, **way out** to **exit**, **present** to **gift**, **rich** to **wealthy**, **break** to **violate**). It is sometimes useful to talk of **human-rights abuses** but often the sentence can be rephrased more pithily and more accurately. **The army is accused of committing numerous human-rights abuses** probably means **The army is accused of torture and murder**.

Avoid, where possible, euphemisms and circumlocutions promoted by interest-groups. The **hearing-impaired** are simply **deaf**. It is no disrespect to the **disabled** sometimes to describe them as

5

crippled. **Female teenagers** are **girls**, not **women**. The **under-privileged** may be **disadvantaged**, but are more likely just **poor**.

And **man** sometimes includes **woman**, just as **he** sometimes makes do for **she** as well. So long as you are not insensitive in other ways, few women will be offended if you do not use **or she** after every he.

> He or she which hath no stomach to this fight,
> Let him or her depart; his or her passport shall be made,
> And crowns for convoy put into his or her purse:
> We would not die in that person's company
> That fears his or her fellowship to die with us.

2. Do not be hectoring or arrogant. Those who disagree with you are not necessarily stupid or insane. Nobody needs to be described as silly: let your analysis prove that he is. When you express opinions, do not simply make assertions. The aim is not just to tell readers what you think, but to persuade them; if you use arguments, reasoning and evidence, you may succeed. Go easy on the oughts and shoulds.

3. Do not be too pleased with yourself. Don't boast of your own cleverness by telling readers that you correctly predicted something or that you have a scoop. You are more likely to bore or irritate them than to impress them. So keep references to *The Economist* to a minimum, particularly those of the we-told-you-so variety. References to "this correspondent" or "your correspondent" are always self-conscious and often self-congratulatory.

4. Do not be too chatty. **Surprise, surprise** is more irritating than informative. So is **Ho, ho**, etc.

5. Do not be too didactic. A recent issue of *The Economist* had an imperative on six out of seven consecutive pages. If too many sentences begin **Compare, Consider, Expect, Imagine, Look at, Note, Prepare for, Remember** or **Take**, readers will think they are reading a textbook (or, indeed, a style book). This may not be the way to persuade them to renew their subscriptions.

6. Do not be sloppy in the construction of your sentences and paragraphs. Do not use a participle unless you make it clear what it applies to. Thus avoid **Having died, they had to bury him**, or **Proceeding along this line of thought, the cause of the train crash becomes clear.**

Don't overdo the use of **don't, isn't, can't, won't**, etc.

Use the subjunctive properly. If you are posing a hypothesis contrary to fact, you must use the subjunctive. Thus, **If Hitler were alive today, he could tell us whether he kept a diary.** If the hypothesis may or may not be true, you do not use the subjunctive: **If this diary is not Hitler's, we shall be glad we did not publish it.** If you have **would** in the main clause, you must use the subjunctive in the if clause. **If you were to disregard this rule, you would make a fool of yourself.**

In general, be concise. Try to be economical in your account or argument ("The best way to be boring is to leave nothing out" – Voltaire). Similarly, try to be economical with words.

Do your best to be lucid. Simple sentences help. Keep complicated constructions and gimmicks to a minimum, if necessary by remembering the *New Yorker*'s comment: "Backward ran sentences until reeled the mind." Mark Twain described how a good writer treats sentences: "At times he may indulge himself with a long one, but he will make sure there are no folds in it, no vaguenesses, no parenthetical interruptions of its view as a whole; when he has done with it, it won't be a sea-serpent with half of its arches under the water; it will be a torch-light procession."

Long paragraphs, like long sentences, can confuse the reader. "The paragraph," according to Fowler, "is essentially a unit of thought, not of length; it must be homogeneous in subject matter and sequential in treatment." One-sentence paragraphs should be used only occasionally.

Clear thinking is the key to clear writing. "A scrupulous writer," observed Orwell, "in every sentence that he writes will ask himself at least four questions, thus: What am I trying to say? What words will express it? What image or idiom will make it clearer? Is this image fresh enough to have an effect? And he will probably ask himself two more: Could I put it more shortly? Have I said anything that is avoidably ugly?"

Scrupulous writers will also notice that their copy is edited only lightly and is likely to be used. It may even be read.

A NOTE ON EDITING

Editing has always made a large contribution to *The Economist*'s excellence. It should continue to do so. But editing on a screen is beguilingly simple. It is quite easy to rewrite an article without realising that one has done much to it at all: the cursor leaves no trace of crossings out, handwritten insertions, rearranged sentences or reordered paragraphs. The temptation is to continue to make changes until something emerges which the editor himself might have written. One benefit of this is a tightly edited newspaper. One cost is a certain sameness. The risk is that the newspaper will turn into a collection of 70 or 80 articles which read as though they have been written by no more than half a dozen hands. *The Economist* has a single editorial outlook, and it is anonymous. But it is the work of many people, both in London and abroad, as its datelines testify. If the prose of our Tokyo correspondent is indistinguishable from the prose of our Nairobi correspondent, readers will feel they are being robbed of variety. They may also wonder whether these two people really exist, or whether the entire newspaper is not written in London. The moral for editors is that they should respect good writing. That is mainly what this style guide is designed to promote. It is not intended to impose a single style on all *The Economist*'s journalists. A writer's style, after all, should reflect his mind and personality. So long as they are compatible with *The Economist*'s, and so long as the prose is good, editors should exercise suitable self-restraint. Remember that your copy, too, will be edited. And even if you think you are not guilty, bear in mind this comment from John Gross:

> Most writers I know have tales to tell of being mangled by editors and mauled by fact-checkers, and naturally it is the flagrant instances they choose to single out – absurdities, outright distortions of meaning, glaring errors. But most of the damage done is a good deal less spectacular. It consists of small changes (usually too boring to describe to anyone else) that flatten a writer's style, slow down his argument, neutralise his irony; that ruin the rhythm of a sentence or the balance of a paragraph; that deaden the tone that makes the music. I sometimes think of the process as one of "de-sophistication".

John Grimond

PART I

THE ESSENCE OF STYLE

A

ABBREVIATIONS. Unless an abbreviation or acronym is so familiar that it is used more often than the full form (eg, BBC, CIA, DNA, EU, FBI, GATT, IMF, NATO, OECD), write the words in full on first appearance: thus **Trades Union Congress** (not TUC). After the first mention, try not to repeat the abbreviation too often; so write **the agency** rather than **the** IAEA, **the Union** rather than **the** EU, to avoid spattering the page with capital letters. There is no need to give the initials of an organisation if it is not referred to again.

If an abbreviation can be pronounced (eg, EFTA, NATO, UNESCO), it does not generally require the definite article. (GATT, however, is sometimes called **the** GATT.) Other organisations, except companies, should usually be preceded by **the** (**the** BBC, **the** NHS, **the** KGB, **the** UNCHR and **the** NIESR). Use MP only after first spelling out Member of Parliament in full (in many places an MP is a military policeman).

Abbreviations that can be pronounced and are composed of bits of words rather than just initials should be spelled out in upper and lower case: **Comecon, Frelimo, Legco, Renamo, Unicef, Unison, Unprofor.** (See also INITIALS.)

In bodymatter, abbreviations, whether they can be pronounced as words or not (GNP, GDP, FOB, CIF, A-**levels**, D-**marks**, T-**shirts**, X-**rays**), should be set in small capitals, with no points – unless they are currencies like **DM** or **FFr**, elements like **H** and **O** or degrees of temperature like °**F** and °**C**. Brackets, apostrophes (see PUNCTUATION) and all other typographical furniture accompanying small capitals are generally set in ordinary roman, with a lower-case s (also roman) for plurals and genitives. Thus IOUs, MPs' salaries, (SDRs), etc. But ampersands are set as small capitals, as are numerals and any hyphens attaching them to a small capital. Thus R&D, A23, M1, F-16, etc. See also AMPERSANDS.

Abbreviations that include upper-case and lower-case letters must be set in a mixture of small capitals and lower case: BAe, BPhil, PhDs.

In headings, rubrics, cross-heads, flytitles, captions, tables, charts (including sources), use ordinary caps, not small caps.

Use lower case for **kg, km, lb** (never **lbs**), **mph** and other MEASURES, and for **ie, eg**, which should both be followed by commas. When used with figures, these lower-case abbreviations should follow immediately, with no space (**11am, 15kg, 35mm, 100mph, 78rpm**), as should AD and BC (76AD, 55BC), though they are set in small capitals. Two abbreviations together, however, must be separated: **60m b/d**.

Most scientific units, except those of temperature, that are named after individuals should be set in small capitals, though any attachments denoting multiples go in lower case. Thus **watt** is **w**, whereas **kilowatt, milliwatt** and **megawatt**, meaning **1,000 watts, one thousandth of a watt** and **1m watts**, are abbreviated to **kw, mw** and MW. The elements do not take small capitals. **Lead** is **Pb, carbon dioxide** is CO_2, **methane** is CH_4. **Chlorofluorocarbons** are, however, CFCs, and the oxides of nitrogen are generally NOX. Different isotopes of the same element are distinguished by raised prefixes: **carbon-14** is ^{14}C, **helium-3** is ^{3}He.

Most upper-case abbreviations take upper-case initial letters when written in full (eg, the LSO is the **London Symphony Orchestra**), but there are exceptions: CAP but **common agricultural policy**, EMU but **economic and monetary union**, GDP but **gross domestic product**, PSBR but **public-sector borrowing requirement**, VLSI but **very large-scale integration**.

Do not use **Prof, Sen, Gen, Col**, etc. **Lieut-Colonel** and **Lieut-Commander** are permissible. So is **Rev**, but it must be preceded by **the** and followed by a Christian name or initial: **the Rev Jesse Jackson** (thereafter **Mr Jackson**).

Always spell out **page, pages, hectares, miles**. But **kilograms** (not **kilogrammes**) and **kilometres** can be shortened to **kg** (or **kilos**) and **km**.

Remember that EFTA is the **European Free Trade Association**, the FAO is the **Food and Agriculture Organisation**, the IDA is the **International Development Association**, the OAU is the **Organisation of African Unity**, the PLO is the **Palestine Liberation Organisation**.

Write **Euro-MPs**, not MEPs.

-ABLE, -EABLE, -IBLE. The following lists are not comprehensive.

-able

debatable	implacable	movable
dispensable	indescribable	tradable
disputable	indictable	unmistakable
forgivable	indispensable	unshakable
imaginable	indistinguishable	

-eable

likeable	rateable	traceable
manageable	serviceable	unpronounceable

-ible

accessible	inadmissible	permissible
convertible	indestructible	submersible
digestible	investible	

ACCENTS. On words now accepted as English, use accents only when they make a crucial difference to pronunciation: **cliché, soupçon, façade, café, communiqué** (but **elite, feted**). If you use one accent, use all: **émigré, mêlée, protégé, résumé.** See also ACCENTS, page 89.

Put the accents and cedillas on French names and words, and umlauts on German ones and tildes (but not other accents) on Spanish ones: **François de Panafieu, Wolfgang Schäuble, Frederico Peña.** In other foreign languages, either use all the accents on proper nouns (names, places, etc) correctly or none.

Any foreign word in italics should, however, be given its proper accents.

ACRONYM: this is a word, like **radar** or NATO, not a set of initials, like the BBC or the IMF.

ACTIVE, NOT PASSIVE. Be direct. **A hit B** describes the event more concisely than **B was hit by A.**

ADVERBS. Put adverbs where you would put them in normal speech which is usually after the verb. But see also AMERICANISMS and PART II.

AFFECT means to have an influence on, as in **The novel affected his attitude to immigrants**. See also EFFECT.

AFFINITY is by definition mutual. It can exist **between** or **with** things, but not **to** or **for** them.

AGGRAVATE means **make worse**, not **irritate** or **annoy**.

AGGRESSION is an unattractive quality, so do not call a **keen** salesman an aggressive one (unless his foot is in the door – or beyond).

AGONY COLUMN: when Sherlock Holmes perused this, it was a **personal column**, not letters to an **agony aunt**.

AGREE: things are agreed **on, to** or **about**, not just agreed.

ALIBI: an **alibi** is the proven fact of being elsewhere, not a false explanation.

ALTERNATE, as an adjective, means **every other**.

ALTERNATIVE: strictly, this is **one of two**, not one of three, four, five or more (which may be **options**).

AMEND is not quite the same as **emend**; though both result in an improvement, **emend** is used only of something written. **He amended his life by giving up gambling and drinking,** but **He emended his memo by correcting the spelling mistakes.**

AMERICANISMS. Use Americanisms discriminatingly. Many American words and expressions have passed into the language; others have vigour, particularly if used occasionally. Some are short and to the point (so prefer **lay off** to **make redundant**). But many are unnecessarily long (so use **and** not **additionally, car** not **automobile, company** not **corporation, transport** not **transportation, district** not **neighbourhood, oblige** not **obligate, stocks** not **inventories** unless there is the risk of confusion with stocks and shares).

Grow a beard or a tomato but not a company. By all means **call for** a record profit if you wish to exhort the workers, but not if you merely predict one. And do not **post** it if it has been achieved. If it has not, look for someone new to **head** it, not to **head it up**.

Try not to verb nouns or to adjective them. So do not **access** files, **haemorrhage** red ink (**haemorrhage** is a noun), let one event **impact** on another, **author** books (still less **co-author** them), **critique** style sheets, **host** parties or **loan** money. **Gunned down** means **shot**.

Choose tenses according to British usage. In particular, do not fight shy of the perfect tense, especially where no date or time is given. Thus **Mr Clinton has woken up to the danger** is preferable

to **Mr Clinton woke up to the danger,** unless you can add **last week** or **when he heard the explosion**.

Americans put the adverbs before the verb; the British put them after, as in normal speech. See also PART II.

AMPERSANDS. Ampersands should be used as follows.
1. When they are part of the name of a company (eg, AT&T, **Pratt & Whitney**).
2. For such things as constituencies where two names are linked to form one unit (eg, **The rest of Brighouse & Spenborough joined with the Batley part of Batley & Morley to form Batley & Spen.** Or **The area thus became the Pakistani province of Kashmir and the Indian state of Jammu & Kashmir**).
3. In R&D, S&L.

AN should be used before a word beginning with a vowel or an h if, and only if, the h is silent. So **a hospital, a hotel**, but **an honorary degree**.

ANARCHY means the **complete absence of law** or government. It may be harmonious or chaotic.

ANIMALS, PLANTS, ETC. When it is necessary to use a Latin name, follow the standard practice. Thus for all creatures higher than viruses, write the binomial name in italics, giving an initial capital to the first word (the genus): *Turdus turdus*, the song thrush; *Metasequoia glyptostroboides*, the dawn redwood.

ANTICIPATE does not mean **expect**. Jack and Jill expected to marry; if they anticipated marriage, only Jill might find herself expectant.

ANY ONE refers to a number; **anyone** to anybody.

ANY WAY refers to any manner; **anyway** means **nevertheless**.

APPEAL is intransitive nowadays (except in America), so **appeal against** decisions.

APPRAISE means **set a price on. Apprise** means **inform**.

AS OF (April 5th or April): prefer **on** (or **after**, or **since**) April 5th, **in** April.

AS TO: there is usually a more appropriate preposition.

AUTARCHY means **absolute sovereignty** but **autarky** means **self-sufficiency**.

B

BALE: in the hayfield, yes, otherwise **bail, bail out**. But **bale out** of a boat.

BEG THE QUESTION means neither **invite the question** nor **evade the answer**. To **beg the question** is to base a conclusion upon an assumption that is as much in need of proof as the conclusion itself.

BIANNUAL can mean **twice a year** or **once every two years**. Avoid.

BIENNIAL means either lasting two years or happening once in two years.

BICENTENNIAL: prefer **bicentenary** (as a noun).

BLACK: in the black means **in profit** in Britain, but **making losses** in some places. Always use **in profit**.

BOTH ... AND: a preposition placed after both should be repeated after and. Thus, **both to right and to left**; but **to both right and left** is all right.

Apply the same rule to **either ... or ...** , **neither ... nor ...** and **not only ... but (also) ...**

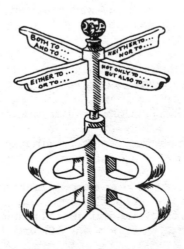

15

C

CANUTE'S exercise on the seashore was designed to persuade his courtiers of what he knew to be true but they doubted, ie, that he was not omnipotent. Don't imply he was surprised to get his feet wet.

CAPITALS.
A balance has to be struck between so many capitals that the eyes dance and so few that the reader is diverted more by our style than by our substance. The general rule is to dignify with capital letters organisations and institutions, but not people. More exact rules are laid out below. Even these, however, leave some decisions to individual judgment. If in doubt use lower case unless it looks absurd. And remember that "a foolish consistency is the hobgoblin of little minds" (Emerson).

1. People. Use upper case for ranks and titles when written in conjunction with a name, but lower case when on their own. Thus, **President Clinton**, but the **president**; **Vice-President Gore**, but the **vice-president**; **Colonel Qaddafi** but the **colonel**; **Pope John Paul**, but the **pope**; **Queen Elizabeth**, but the **queen**.

Do not write **Prime Minister Major** or **Defence Secretary Perry**; they are the **prime minister**, **Mr Major**, and the **defence secretary**, **Mr Perry**. You may, however, write **Chancellor Kohl**.

All office holders when referred to merely by their office, not by their name, are lower case: the **chancellor of the exchequer**, the **foreign secretary**, the **prime minister**, the **speaker**, the **treasury secretary**, the **president of the United States**, the **chairman of British Airways**.

The only exceptions are: (a) a few titles that would look unduly peculiar without capitals, eg, **Black Rod**, **Master of the Rolls**, **Chancellor of the Duchy of Lancaster**, **Lord Privy Seal**, **Lord Chancellor**; (b) a few exalted people, such as the **Dalai Lama**, the **Aga Khan**. Also **God**. See also TITLES.

2. Organisations, ministries, departments, treaties, acts, etc, generally take upper case when their full name (or something pretty close to it, eg, **State Department**) is used. Thus, **European Commission**, **Forestry Commission**, **Arab League**, **Amnesty International**, the **Household Cavalry**, **Ministry of Agriculture**, **Department of Trade and Industry**, **Treasury**, **Metropolitan Police**, **High Court**, **Supreme Court**, **Court of Appeal**, **Senate**,

Central Committee, Politburo, Oxford University, the New York Stock Exchange (but the London stock exchange, since that is only its informal name), the Treaty of Rome, the Health and Safety at Work Act, etc.

So, too, the House of Commons, House of Lords, House of Representatives, St Paul's Cathedral (the cathedral), World Bank (the Bank), Bank of England (the Bank), Department of State (the department).

But organisations, committees, commissions, special groups, etc, that are either impermanent, ad hoc, local or relatively insignificant should be lower case. Thus: the subcommittee on journalists' rights of the National Executive Committee of the Labour Party, the international economic subcommittee of the Senate Foreign Relations Committee, the Oxford University bowls club, Market Blandings rural district council.

Use lower case for rough descriptions (the safety act, the American health department, the French parliament, as distinct from its National Assembly). If you are not sure whether the English translation of a foreign name is exact or not, assume it is rough and use lower case.

Parliament and Congress are upper case. But the opposition is lower case, even when used in the sense of her majesty's loyal opposition. The government, the administration and the cabinet are always lower case.

3. The full name of political parties is upper case, including the word party: Republican Party, Labour Party, Peasants' Party. Note that only people are Democrats, Christian Democrats, Liberal Democrats or Social Democrats; their parties, policies, committees, etc, are Democratic, Christian Democratic, Liberal Democratic or Social Democratic (although a committee may be Democrat-controlled).

When referring to a specific party, write Labour, the Republican nominee, a prominent Liberal, etc, but use lower case in looser references to liberals, conservatism, communists, etc. Tories, however, are upper case.

4. A political, economic or religious label formed from a proper name, eg, Gaullism, Paisleyite, Leninist, Napoleonic, Jacobite, Luddite, Marxist, Hobbesian, Christian, Buddhism, Hindu, Maronite, Finlandisation, Thatcherism, should have a capital.

5. In finance and government there are some particular exceptions to the general rule of initial caps for full names, lower case for informal ones. Use caps for the World Bank and the Fed (after first spelling it out as the Federal Reserve), although these are shortened, informal names. The Bank of England and its foreign equiva-

lents have initial caps when named formally and separately, but collectively they are central banks in lower case (except Ireland's, which is actually named the **Central Bank**). **Special drawing rights** are lower case but abbreviated in small caps as SDRs, except when used with a figure as a currency (**SDR500m**). **Deutschemarks** are usually just D-marks. Treasury bonds issued by America's Treasury should be upper case; treasury bills (or bonds) of a general kind should be lower case. Avoid **T-bonds** and **t-bills**.

After first mention, the **House of Commons** (or **Lords**, or **Representatives**) becomes the **House**, the **World Bank** and **Bank of England** become the **Bank** and the IMF can become the **Fund**. Organisations with unusual names, such as the **African National Congress, Civic Forum** and the **European Union**, become the **Congress**, the **Forum** and the **Union**. But most other organisations – agencies, banks, commissions (including the **European Commission**), etc – take lower case when referred to incompletely on second mention.

6. Places. Use initial capitals for definite geographical places, regions, areas and countries (**The Hague, Transylvania, Germany**), and for vague but recognised political or geographical areas: the **Middle East, South Atlantic, East Asia** (which is to be preferred to the **Far East**), the **West** (as in the decline of the West), the **Gulf, North Atlantic, South-East Asia,** the **Midlands, Central America,** the **West Country, Western Europe.**

Use lower case for **east, west, north, south** except when part of a name (**North Korea, South Africa, West End**) or when part of a thinking group: the **South** (in the United States), the **Highlands** (of Scotland). But use lower case if you are, say, comparing regions of the United States, some of which are merely geographical areas: **House prices in the north-east and the south are rising faster than those in the mid-west and the south-west.**

Use **West Germany (Berlin)** and **East Germany (Berlin)** only in historical references. They are now **western Germany (western Berlin)** and **eastern Germany (eastern Berlin)**.

The **third world** (an unsatisfactory term now that the communist second world has disappeared) is lower case.

If in doubt, use lower case (**the sunbelt**).

Use capitals for particular buildings, even if the name is not strictly accurate (eg, the **Foreign Office**).

Use lower case for province, county, state, city when not strictly part of the name: **Washington state, Cabanas province, Guatemala city, Kuwait city, New York city, Panama city, Quebec city** (but **Dodge City, Ho Chi Minh City, Kansas City, Oklahoma City, Quezon City, Salt Lake City**).

7. Use capitals to avoid confusion, especially with no (and therefore yes). **In Bergen no votes predominated** suggests a stalemate, whereas **In Bergen No votes predominated** suggests a triumph of noes over yeses. In most contexts, though, yes and no should be lower case: "The answer is no."

8. Others

Some political terms (upper case)

Communist	the Crown	Tory
(if a particular party)	Parliament	Warsaw Pact
Congress	Teamster	

Historical periods (upper case)

Black Death	Renaissance
the Depression	Restoration
Middle Ages	Year of the Dog (but new year
New Deal	and new year's day)
Reconstruction	

Trade names (upper case)
Hoover, Teflon, Valium, etc

Miscellaneous (upper case)

anti-Semitism	Mafia (the genuine article)
the Bar	Pershing missile
Catholics	Protestants
the Cup Final	Pyrrhic
the Davis Cup	Sandinist (not Sandinista)
Eurobond	Semitic (-ism)
Euroyen bond	Stealth fighter, bomber, missile
Hispanics	Test match
House of Laity	Utopia (-n)
Internet	Young Turks

Miscellaneous (lower case)

19th amendment	cruise missile	the pope
(but Article19)	cultural revolution	the press
aborigines	e-mail	the queen
administration	french windows	realpolitik
angst	general synod	the right
blacks	government	the shah
cabinet	the left	the speaker
civil servant	mafia (any old group	the sunbelt
civil service	of criminals)	third world
common market	new year	state-of-the-union
communist (generally)	new year's day	message
constitution	opposition	white paper

CARTEL. A cartel is a group that restricts supply in order to drive up prices. Do not use it to describe any old syndicate or association of producers.

CASE: "There is perhaps no single word so freely resorted to as a trouble-saver," says Gowers, "and consequently responsible for so much flabby writing." Often you can do without it. **There are many cases of it being unnecessary** is better as **It is often unnecessary. If it is the case that** ... simply means **If. It is not the case** means **It is not so.**

CASSANDRA'S predictions were correct but not believed.

CATALYST: this is something that speeds up a chemical reaction while itself remaining unchanged. Do not confuse it with one of the agents.

CENSOR. The critics may **censure** a bad play, but oppose any attempt to **censor** it, that is **suppress all or part** of it.

CENTRED on, not **around** or **in**.

CHARGE: if you **charge** intransitively, do so as a bull, cavalry officer or some such, not as an **accuser** (so avoid **The standard of writing was abysmal, he charged**).

CIRCUMSTANCES stand **around** a thing, so it is **in**, not **under**, them.

COIFFED, not **coiffured**.

COLLAPSE is not transitive. You may collapse, but you may not collapse something.

COLLECTIVE NOUNS. There is no firm rule about the number of a verb governed by a singular collective noun. It is best to go by the sense, ie, whether the collective noun stands for a single entity (**The council was elected in March, The me generation has run its course, The staff is loyal**) or for its constituents (**The council are at sixes and sevens over taxes, The preceding generation are all dead, The staff are at each other's throats**).
A rule for **number: The number is** ... , **A number are** ...
A **pair** and a **couple** are both plural.
A rule for **majority**. When it is used in an abstract sense, it takes the singular; when it is used to denote the elements making up the majority, it should be plural. **A two-thirds majority is needed to amend the constitution** but **A majority of the Senate were opposed.**

A **government**, a **party**, a **company** (whether Tesco or Marks and Spencer) and a **partnership** (Skidmore, Owings & Merrill) are all **it**, and take a singular verb. So does a **country**, even if its name looks plural. Thus **The United States is helping the Philippines**. **The United Nations** is singular. **Politics** is also singular; so are **economics**, **mechanics** and **physics** – though not **antics**, nor **statistics**.

Brokers too. **Legg Mason Wood Walk is preparing a statement**. Avoid **stockbrokers Furman Selz Mager, bankers Chase Manhattan** or **accountants Ernst & Young**. And remember that **Barclays is a British bank, not the British bank**, just as **Ford is a car company**, not **the car company** and **Luciano Pavarotti is an opera singer**, not **the opera singer**.

Some nouns ending in **s** are always treated as singular; they include **news** and games such as **darts, bowls** and **billiards**.

Law and order defies the rules of grammar and is singular.

COME UP WITH: try **suggest, originate** or **produce**.

COMPANIES.
Call companies by the names they call themselves.

Airbus Industrie
Aérospatiale
Allied-Domecq
American Telephone and
  Telegraph (AT&T)
Anglo American
Banc One
B.A.T Industries
Bayerische Hypotheken- und
  Wechsel-Bank (space before
  the und, no hyphen after)
Bloomingdale's
Boots (the chemist)
British Aerospace (BAe)
BSkyB
Cadbury Schweppes
W.I. Carr (sometimes known
  as WICO)
casa (Spanish Airbus partner;
  not Construcciones
  Aeronauticas SA in full)
Coca-Cola
Compaq
Consolidated Gold Fields
County NatWest

Cummins Engine
Donaldson, Lufkin & Jenrette
Du Pont
Eastman Kodak
Ernst & Young
Fried. Krupp
Glaxo Wellcome
Goldman Sachs
Hamleys
Hanson (not Trust)
Hanson Industries
  (the American arm)
Harrods
Hewlett-Packard
Hoare Govett
Hongkong & Shanghai Bank
  (but more likely
  HSBC Holdings)
Japan Airlines
Kohlberg Kravis Roberts
Kraft Foods
Lloyd's (insurance market)
Lloyds Bank
Lord & Taylor
McDonald's

McDonnell Douglas
Marks and Spencer plc (but
  Marks & Spencer is the
  name above the shop)
Merrell
Merrill Lynch
Messerschmitt-Bölkow-Blohm
  (MBB)
Moët & Chandon
Moody's
J.P. Morgan
Motoren Turbine Union (MTU)
next (Steve Jobs's computer
  firm, *not* Britain's retailer)
Nippon Telegraph and
  Telephone (NTT)
Olympia & York
Philips
Pillsbury
PolyGram
Pratt & Whitney
Procter & Gamble

Ranks Hovis McDougall
Rich's
Rolls-Royce (cars and
  aero engines)
Saks Fifth Avenue
savings and loan associations
  (*not* loans)
Sears, Roebuck
Shearson Lehman Hutton
Short Brothers
SmithKline Beecham
Smith New Court
Standard & Poor's
Thorn EMI
Time Warner
Tonen Corporation (formerly
  Toa Nenryo)
UBS
Unix
S.G. Warburg
Zeneca

Some other British and American company names are listed under
STOCK MARKET INDICES (see pages 138ff).

COMPARE: A is compared **with** B when you draw attention to the
difference. A is compared **to** B when you want to stress their similar-
ity ("Shall I compare thee to a summer's day?")

COMPLAISANT people aim to please others; if they are **compla-
cent**, they are pleased with themselves.

COMPOUND does not mean **make worse**. It may mean **combine**
or, intransitively, **agree** or **come to terms**. To **compound a felony**
means to **agree for a consideration not to prosecute**.

COMPRISE means **is composed of**. The Democratic coalition
comprises women, workers, blacks and Jews. Women make
up (not comprise) three-fifths of the Democratic coalition.
Alternatively, **Three-fifths of the Democratic coalition is composed of women**.

CONTINUOUS describes something uninterrupted; **continual**
admits of a break. If your neighbours play loud music every night, it
is a **continual nuisance**; but it isn't a **continuous nuisance** unless
the music is never turned off.

CONVINCE. Don't **convince** people to do something. In that context the word you want is **persuade**. **The prime minister was persuaded to call a June election; he was convinced of the wisdom of doing so only after he had won.**

COUNTRIES AND THEIR INHABITANTS. In most contexts sacrifice precision to simplicity and use **Britain** rather than **Great Britain** or the **United Kingdom,** and **America** rather than the **United States of America.** ("In all pointed sentences some degree of accuracy must be sacrificed to conciseness." Dr Johnson.) (See also pages 133ff.)

It is sometimes important to be precise in other contexts. Remember therefore that **Great Britain** consists of **England, Scotland** and **Wales,** which together with **Northern Ireland** (which we generally call **Ulster,** though Ulster strictly includes three counties in the republic of Ireland) make up the **United Kingdom.**

Ireland is simply **Ireland.** Although it is a republic, it is not the Republic of Ireland. Neither is it, in English, Eire.

Holland, though a nice, short, familiar name, is strictly only two of the 11 provinces that make up **the Netherlands,** and the **Dutch** are increasingly indignant about misuse of the shorter name. So use **the Netherlands.**

The primary definition of **Scandinavia** is Norway and Sweden, but it is often used to include Denmark, Iceland, Norway and Sweden, which, with Finland, make up the **Nordic countries.**

Where countries have made it clear that they wish to be called by a new (or an old) name, respect their requests. Thus **Côte d'Ivoire, Myanmar,** etc, awkward as they are, along with **Burkina Faso, Sri Lanka, Thailand, Zimbabwe,** etc.

The former **Soviet Union** used often to be called **Russia,** particularly in foreign-policy contexts. But nowadays Russia is only one of the countries that make up the COMMONWEALTH OF INDEPENDENT STATES. Some names of republics of the former Soviet Union have been changed; for instance, Moldavia is now Moldova, Belorussia is Belarus. Some city names have also changed: Leningrad is now St Petersburg and Gorky has become Nizhny Novgorod.

Remember, too, that although it is usually all right to talk about the inhabitants of the United States as **Americans,** the term also applies to everyone from Canada to Cape Horn. It may sometimes be necessary to write **United States citizens.** Do not, however, use **US,** except where it is part of a company's name, when it should be small caps.

In all cases it is best to refer to the specific nationality: thus **Canadians** rather than **North Americans.**

CREDIBLE **means to be believable; credulous means too ready to believe. Her explanation for missing the meeting was credible. His explanation that he found the money at the end of the rainbow convinced only the credulous.**

CRESCENDO. This is not an acme, apogee, peak, summit or zenith but a **passage of increasing loudness**. You cannot therefore **build to a crescendo**.

CRISIS. This is a decisive event or turning-point. Many of the economic and political troubles wrongly described as **crises** are really **persistent difficulties, sagas** or **affairs**.

CURRENCIES. Use $ as the standard currency and in general convert currencies to $ on first mention.

Britain

lp, 2p, 3p, to **99p** (*not* £0.99)	**£5m–6m** (*not* £5m–£6m)
£6 (*not* £6.00)	**£5 billion–6 billion**
£5,000–6000 (*not* £5,000–£6,000)	(*not* £5–6 billion)

A **billion** is a thousand million, a **trillion** is a thousand billion. See also FIGURES, MEASUREMENT and MEASURES (Part III, pages 115ff).

America
$ will do generally. Spell out **cents**.

A$, C$, HK$, M$, NT$, NZ$ and **S$** are Australian, Canadian, Hong Kong, Malaysian, New Taiwanese, New Zealand and Singapore $ or dollars. Other currencies are **DM, BFr, FFr, SFr, IR£** (punts), **ASch, Pta, SDR, DKr** (Danish krone, kroner), **NKr** (Norwegian krone, kroner), **SKr** (Swedish krona, kronor) and **Y**. With all these, write the abbreviation followed by the figure: **Y100** (not 100 yen), **Pta100** (not 100 pesetas), **SDR lm** (not lm SDRs).

Sums in other currencies, including the **ecu**, are written in full, with the number first: **100m ecus, 100m escudos, 100m guilders, 100m kwacha, 100m lire** (if Italian, **liras** if Turkish), **100m naira, 100m pesos, 100m rand** (not rands), **100m rupees** and **100m yuan** (not renminbi). To avoid confusion the *real* is set in italics.

Currencies are not set in small caps, unless they occur as words in text without figures attached: **He who pays the piper, whether in** D-marks or SDRs, **calls the tune.**

For a full list of currencies, with currency symbols (included for reference, not necessarily for use), see pages 101ff.

CURRENT and **contemporary** mean **at that time**, not necessarily **at this time**. So a series of **current prices** from 1960 to 1970 will not be in **today's prices,** just as **contemporary art** in 1800 was not **modern art. Contemporary history** is a contradiction in terms.

D

DATES. Month, day, year, in that order, with no commas:

July 5th	July 1998
Monday July 5th	1990s
July 5th 1998	July 27th–August 3rd 1998
July 5th–12th 1998	1998–99

Write out
20th century, 21st century   **20th-century ideas**
but
a man in his 20s, and **20th anniversary**.

In general give dates; **last week** or **last month** can cause confusion.
    Write **the second world war** or **the 1939–45 war**, not **world war two, II** or **2**. Similarly, prefer **the first world war** to **world war I** or **1. Post-war** and **pre-war** are hyphenated.
    See also FIGURES and HYPHENS.

DECIMATE means to destroy a proportion (originally a tenth) of a group of people or things, not to destroy them all or nearly all.

DEFINITIVE means authoritative, final, decisive; **definite** means precise, distinct.

DELIVER is transitive. So if someone is to **deliver**, he must deliver **letters, babies** or **the goods** – whether **groceries** or **what he promised**.

DEPRECATE means to **express disapproval of; depreciate** means to **belittle** or **reduce the value of. They deprecated his violent language but did not wish to depreciate the importance of his message.**

DIFFERENT from, not **to** or **than**.

DILEMMA. This is not just any old awkwardness, it is one with horns, being, properly, a form of argument (the horned syllogism) in which you find yourself committed to accept one of two propositions each of which contradicts your original contention. Hence a dilemma offers the choice between alternatives, each with equally nasty consequences.

DISCREET means **circumspect** or **prudent**; discrete means **separate** or **distinct**. Remember that **"Questions are never indiscreet. Answers sometimes are."** (Oscar Wilde)

DISINTERESTED means **impartial**; uninterested means **bored**. (**"Disinterested curiosity is the lifeblood of civilisation."** G.M. Trevelyan.)

DISTINCTIVE means **characteristic, serving to identify**; distinct means **definite, distinguishable, separate. Entering his room, she noticed that, as well as the distinctive smell of the cigars he always smoked, there was a faint but distinct odour of rotting fish.**

DUE TO has three meanings:
1. caused by, as in **The cancellation, due to rain, of ...** In this sense, it must follow a noun, so do not write **The match was cancelled due to rain.** If you mean **because of** and for some reason are reluctant to say it, you probably want **owing to. It was cancelled owing to rain** is all right.
2. owed to, as in **A month's salary is due to Smith.**
3. arranged or timed to, as in **The meeting is due to end at 3.30.**

E

-EABLE. See -ABLE.

EARNINGS: do not write **earnings** when you mean **profits** (say if they are operating, gross, pre-tax or net).

-EE: employees, evacuees, detainees, referees, refugees but, please, no **attendees** (those attending), **draftees** (conscripts), **escapees** (escapers) or **retirees** (the retired).

EFFECT means to **accomplish**, so **The novel effected a change in his attitude.** See also AFFECT.

EFFECTIVELY means **with effect**; if you mean **in effect**, say it. **The matter was effectively dealt with on Friday** means it was **done well** on Friday. **The matter was, in effect, dealt with on Friday** means that it was **more or less attended to** on Friday. **Effectively leaderless** would do as a description of the demonstrators in East Germany in 1989 but not those in Tiananmen Square. The devaluation of the Slovak currency in 1993, described by some as an **effective** 8%, turned out to be a rather ineffective 8%.

ENORMITY means a **crime, sin** or **monstrous wickedness.** It does not mean immensity.

EPICENTRE means that point on the earth's surface above the centre of an earthquake. To say that **Mr Jones was at the epicentre of the dispute** suggests that the argument took place underground.

ETHNIC GROUPS. Avoid giving offence. This should be your first concern. But also avoid mealy-mouthed euphemisms and terms that

have not generally caught on despite promotion by pressure-groups. If and when it becomes plain that American blacks no longer wish to be called **black**, as some years ago it became plain that they no longer wished to be called **coloured**, then call them **African-American** (or whatever). Till then they are **blacks**.

When writing about Spanish-speaking people in the United States, use either **Latino** or **Hispanic** as a general term, but try to be specific (eg, Mexican-American).

Africans may be black or white. If you mean blacks, write **blacks**. People of mixed race in South Africa are **Coloureds**.

The inhabitants of **Azerbaijan** are **Azerbaijanis**, some of whom, but not all, are **Azeris**. Those **Azeris** who live in other places, such as Nakhichevan, are not **Azerbaijanis**.

Anglo-Saxon is not a synonym for English-speaking.

See also STATES, Part III, pages 133ff.

EVERY ONE refers to a number; **everyone** means **everybody**.

EX. Be careful with **ex: a Liberal ex-member** has lost his seat; **an ex-Liberal member** has lost his party.

EXCEPTIONABLE means **can be taken exception to**; exceptional means **unusual, out of the ordinary**. To claim that there has been no musical genius since Beethoven is an exceptionable remark, as there have been many other exceptional composers.

F

FACT. **The fact that** can usually be boiled down to **that.**

FEWER (not **less**) **than seven speeches, fewer than seven samurai.** Use **fewer,** not **less,** with numbers of individual items or people. **Less than £200, less than 700 tonnes of oil, less than a third,** because these are measured quantities or proportions, not individual items.

FIEF, not **fiefdom.**

FIGURES.
Never start a sentence with a figure; write the number in words instead.

Use figures for numerals from 11 upwards, and for all numerals that include a decimal point or a fraction (eg, **4.25, 4¼).** Use words for simple numerals from one to ten, except: in references to pages; in percentages (eg, **4%);** and in sets of numerals some of which are higher than ten, eg, **Deaths from this cause in the past three years were 14, 9 and 6.** It is occasionally permissible to use words rather than numbers when referring to a rough or rhetorical figure (such as **a thousand curses).**

Fractions should be hyphenated (**two-thirds, five-eighths,** etc) and, unless they are attached to whole numbers (**8½, 29⅝),** spelled out in words, even when the figures are higher than ten: **He gave a tenth of his salary to the church, a twentieth to his mistress and a thirtieth to his wife.** See also FRACTIONS, page 108.

Do not compare a fraction with a decimal (so avoid **The rate fell from 3½% to 3.1%).**

Fractions are more precise than decimals (3.14 neglects an infinity of figures that are embraced by $^{22}/_7$), but your readers probably do not think so. You should therefore use fractions for rough figures (**Kenya's population is growing at 3½% a year, A hectare is 2½ acres**) and decimals for more exact ones: **The retail price index is rising at an annual rate of 10.6%.** Treat all numbers with respect but beware of phoney over-precision.

Use **m** for **million.** But spell out **billion,** which to us means 1,000m, except in charts, where **bn** is permissible. Thus: **8m, £8m, 8 billion, DM8 billion.**

Use **5,000–6,000, 5–6%, 5m–6m** (not **5–6m)** and also **5 billion–6 billion** or **5bn–6bn.** But **sales rose from 5m to 6m** (not **5m–6m); estimates ranged between 5m and 6m** (not **5m–6m).**

Where **to** is being used as part of a ratio, it is usually best to spell it out. Thus **They decided, by nine votes to two, to put the matter to the general assembly which voted, 27 to 19, to insist that the ratio of vodka to tomato juice in a bloody mary should be at least one to three, though the odds of this being so in most bars were put at no better than 11 to 4.** Where a ratio is being used adjectivally, figures and hyphens may be used, but only if one of the figures is greater than ten: thus a **50-20 vote, a 19-9 vote.** Otherwise, spell out the figures and use **to: a two-to-one vote, a ten-to-one likelihood.**

Do not use a hyphen or dash in place of **to** except with figures: **He received a sentence of 15–20 years in jail** but **He promised to have escaped within three to four weeks' time.**

Avoid **from 1947–50** (say **in 1947–50** or **from 1947 to 1950**) and **between 1961–65** (say **in 1961–65** or **from 1961 to 1965**).

With figures, use **a person** or **per person, a year** or **per year**, not **per caput, per capita** or **per annum.**

The style for aircraft types can be confusing. Some have hyphens in obvious places (eg, F-22, B-2 **bomber**), some in unusual places (MiG 31M) and some none at all (**Airbus** A340, **BAe**, RJ70). Others have both name and number (**Lockheed** P-3 **Orion**). When in doubt, use Jane's "All The World's Aircraft". Its index also includes makers' correct names.

The style for calibres is **50mm** or **105mm** with no hyphen, but **5.5-inch** and **25-pounder.**

Use the sign % instead of **per cent**. But write **percentage**, not **%age** (though in most contexts **proportion** or **share** is preferable).

See also HYPHENS, MEASUREMENTS, MEASURES (Part III, page 115ff).

FINALLY: do not use **finally** when, at the end of a series, you mean **lastly** or, in other contexts, when you mean **at last**. **Richard Burton finally marries Liz Taylor** would have been all right second time round but not first.

FLAUNT means **display**; **flout** means **disdain**. If you **flout** this distinction you will **flaunt** your ignorance.

FOREIGN WORDS AND PHRASES. Try not to use foreign words and phrases unless there is no English alternative, which is unusual (so **a year** or **per year**, not **per annum; a person** or **per person** not **per capita; beyond one's authority** not **ultra vires**; etc). See also ITALICS.

FORGO means **do without;** it forgoes the **e. Forego** means **go before. A foregone conclusion** is one that is predetermined; **a forgone conclusion** is non-existent.

FORMER: avoid wherever possible use of **the former** and **the latter**. It usually causes confusion.

FORTUITOUS means **accidental,** not **fortunate** or **well-timed.**

FRACTIOUS means **peevish** or **unruly; factious** means **divisive** or produced by **faction. English soccer fans have a reputation for being both fractious and factious.**

FRANKENSTEIN was not a monster, but his creator.

FREE is an adjective or an adverb, so you cannot have or do anything **for free.** Either you have it **free** or you have it **for nothing.**

FUND is a technical term, meaning to **convert floating debt into more or less permanent debt at fixed interest.** Do not use it if you mean to **finance** or to **pay for.**

G

GENDER is a word to be applied to grammar, not people. If someone is female, that is her **sex** not her **gender**.

GENERATION: take care. You can be a second-generation Frenchman, but if you are a second-generation immigrant that means you have left the country your parents came to.

GENITIVE. Take care with the genitive. It is fine to say **a friend of Bill's**, just as you would say **a friend of mine**, so you can also say **a friend of Bill's and Hillary's**. But it is also fine to say **a friend of Bill**, or **a friend of Bill and Hillary**. What you must not say is **Bill and Hillary's friend**. If you wish to use that construction, you must say **Bill's and Hillary's friend**, which is cumbersome.

GENTLEMEN'S AGREEMENT, not **gentleman's**.

GERUND. Respect the gerund. Gerunds look like participles – **running, jumping, standing** – but are more noun-like, and should never therefore be preceded by a personal pronoun. So the following are wrong: **I was awoken by him snoring. He could not prevent them drowning. Please forgive me coming late.** Those sentences should have ended: **his snoring, their drowning, my coming late.** In other words, use the possessive adjective rather than the personal pronoun.

GET: an adaptable verb, but it has its limits. A man does not **get** sacked or promoted, he **is** sacked or promoted.

GOURMET means **epicure**; gourmand means **greedy-guts**.

H

HALVE is a transitive verb, so deficits can double but not **halve**. They must **be halved** or **fall by half**.

HANGING CLAUSES. If you begin a sentence with an adjectival or adverbial phrase, make sure that it qualifies the subject of the sentence. Thus, avoid: **After a fortnight's absence, your house plants will have shrivelled up.**

HEALTHY. If you think something is **desirable** or **good**, say so. Do not call it **healthy**.

HOBSON'S CHOICE is not **the lesser of two evils**, it is **no choice at all**.

HOI POLLOI means **the many** or **the rabble** in Greek. Do not therefore write **the hoi polloi**.

HOMOGENEOUS means **of the same kind or nature**. **Homogenous** means **similar because of common descent**.

HOMOSEXUAL: since this word comes from the Greek word *homos* (same), not the Latin word *homo* (man), it applies as much to women as to men. It is therefore as daft to write **homosexuals and lesbians** as to write **people and women**.

HOPEFULLY: by all means begin an article hopefully, but never write: **Hopefully, it will be finished by Wednesday.** Try: **With luck, if all goes well, it is hoped that ...**

HYPHENS.
Use hyphens as follows.

1. Fractions (whether nouns or adjectives): **two-thirds, four-fifths, one-sixth,** etc. (See also FRACTIONS, Part III, page 108.)

2. Most words that begin with prefixes like **ex, anti, non** and **neo**. Thus, **anti-aircraft, anti-fascist, anti-submarine** (but anticlimax, antidote, antiseptic); **non-combatant, non-existent, non-payment, non-violent** (but nonaligned, nonconformist, nonplussed, nonstop); **neo-conservative, neo-liberal** (but neoclassicism, neolithic, neologism).

Words beginning **Euro** should also be hyphenated, except **Europhile, Europhobe** and **Eurosceptic**.

Some words that become unmanageably long with the addition of a prefix. Thus **under-secretary** and **inter-governmental**. **Antidisestablishmentarianism** would, however, lose its point it if were hyphenated.

A sum followed by the word **worth** also needs a hyphen: thus, **$25m-worth of goods**.

3. Some titles:

vice-president	*but*
director-general	**deputy director**
under-secretary	**deputy secretary**
secretary-general	**district attorney**
attorney-general	**general secretary**
lieutenant-colonel	
major-general	

4. To avoid ambiguities:

a little-used car	**a little used-car**
cross-complaint	**cross complaint**
high-school girl	**high schoolgirl**

fine-tooth comb (most people do not comb their teeth)

5. Adjectives formed from two or more words:
right-wing groups (*but* **the right wing** of the party)
balance-of-payments difficulties
private-sector wages
public-sector borrowing requirement
a 70-year-old judge
value-added tax (VAT)

6. Adverbs do not need to be linked to participles or adjectives by hyphens in simple constructions: **The regiment was ill equipped for its task; The principle is well established; Though expensively educated, the journalist knew no grammar.** But if the adverb is one of two words together being used adjectivally, a hyphen may be needed: **The ill-equipped regiment was soon repulsed; All well-established principles should be periodically challenged.** The hyphen is especially likely to be needed if the adverb is short and common, such as **ill, little, much** and **well**. Less-common adverbs, including all those that end -ly, are less likely to need hyphens: **Never employ an expensively educated journalist.** See ADVERBS.

7. Do not overdo the literary device of hyphenating words that are not usually linked: the stringing-together-of-lots-and-lots-of-words-

and-ideas tendency can be tiresome.

8. Separating identical letters: **book-keeping** (but **bookseller**), **coat-tails, co-operate, unco-operative, pre-eminent, pre-empt** (but **predate, precondition**), **re-emerge, re-entry, trans-ship.** But **rearrange, reborn, repurchase.** Exceptions also include **override, overrule, underrate, withhold.**

9. Nouns formed from prepositional verbs: **bail-out, build-up, call-up, get-together, round-up, set-up, shake-up,** etc.

10. The quarters of the compass: **north-east(ern), south-east(ern), south-west(ern), north-west(ern), the mid-west(ern).**

11. Makers, miners, workers can stand unattached and hyphenless: **car maker, coal miner, steel worker.** But **policy-makers, policy-making.**

12. *One word*

airfield	headache	seabed
antibiotic	hijack	shipbuilders
anticlimax	hobnob	shortlist
antidote	kowtow	soyabean
antiseptic	lacklustre	stockmarket
antitrust	loophole	strongman
backlog	lopsided	subcommittee
bilingual	lukewarm	subcontinent
blackboard	multilingual	subcontract
blueprint	nationwide	subhuman
businessman	nevertheless	sunbelt
bypass	nonetheless	takeover
ceasefire	offshore	taskforce
coastguard	oilfield	threshold
comeback	onshore	turnout
commonsense (adj)	overpaid	underdog
figleaf	overrated	underpaid
foothold	override	underrated
forever	overrule	videocassette
goodwill	peacekeepers (-ing)	videodisc
halfhearted	petrochemical	wartime
handout	profitmaking	workforce
handpicked	rainforest	worldwide
hardline	salesforce	worthwhile

13. *Two words*

air base	aircraft carrier	ballot box
air force	arm's length	car maker

chip maker
coal miner
common sense
  (noun)
drug dealer (-ing)

errand boy
girl friend
health care
microchip maker
on to

steel maker
steel worker
under way
vice versa

14. *Two hyphenated words*

agri-business
asylum-seekers
build-up
death-squads
drawing-board
end-game
end-year
faint-hearted
fund-raiser (-ing)
heir-apparent
hot-head
ice-cream
infra-red

know-how
mid-week, mid-
  August, etc
nation-state
policy-makers
  (-ing), *but*
  foreign-policy
  makers (-ing)
post-war
pre-war
pull-out (noun)
re-create (*meaning*
  create again)

re-present (*meaning*
  present again)
re-sort (*meaning*
  sort again)
starting-point
sticking-point
talking-shop
task-force
think-tank
time-bomb
turning-point
working-party

15. *Three words*

ad hoc agreement
capital gains tax
chiefs of staff
in as much
in so far

Three hyphenated words

brother-in-law
chock-a-block
commander-in-chief
no-man's-land
prisoners-of-war
second-in-command

16. Avoid **from 1947–50** (say **in 1947–50** or **from 1947 to 1950**) and **between 1961–65** (say **in 1961–65** or **from 1961 to 1965**). Some people use dashes, not hyphens, with dates. A hyphen (or dash) should not be used instead of **to** except with figures. See also DATES, FIGURES.

HYPOTHERMIA is what kills old folk in winter. If you say it is **hyperthermia,** that means they have been carried off by heat stroke.

I

-IBLE. See -ABLE.

ILK means **same,** so **of that ilk** means **of the place of the same name as the family,** not **of that kind.** Best avoided.

IMMOLATE means to **sacrifice,** not to **burn.**

IMPORTANT: if something is important, say why and to whom. Use sparingly.

INCHOATE means **not fully developed** or **at an early stage,** and not **incoherent** or **chaotic.**

INFER. By including this word, we **imply** that it is sometimes misused. When reading this entry, you **infer** that the two highlighted words have different meanings.

INITIALS. Initials in people's names, or in companies named after them, take points (with a space between initials and name, but not between initials). Thus, **F.W. de Klerk, E.I. Du Pont de Nemours, F.W. Woolworth.** The only exceptions are for PEOPLE, COMPANIES and ORGANISATIONS that deliberately leave the points out. In general, follow the practice preferred by themselves in writing their own names. See also ABBREVIATIONS.

INTERNMENT. Generally considered a preferable penalty to **interment**: the former means **confinement,** the latter means **burial** in a grave or tomb.

INVESTIGATIONS **of,** not **into.**

ITALICS. Use italics for:

1. Foreign words and phrases, such as *cabinet* (French type), *de jure, glasnost, intifada, Mitbestimmung, papabile, perestroika, ujamaa* unless they are so familiar that they have become anglicised. Thus **ad hoc, apartheid, machismo, putsch, pogrom, realpolitik, status quo,** etc, are in roman. Make sure that the meaning of any foreign word you use is clear; and give it its correct accents. See also ACCENTS; ANIMALS, PLANTS, ETC; FOREIGN WORDS AND PHRASES.

2. Newspapers and periodicals. Note that only *The Economist* and *The Times* have **The** italicised. Thus the *Daily Telegraph*, the *New York Times*, the *Observer*, the *Spectator*, the *Independent*, the *Financial Times* (but *Le Monde, Die Welt, Die Zeit*). Books, pamphlets, plays, radio and television programmes are roman, with capital letters for each main word, in quotation marks. Thus: **"Pride and Prejudice", "Much Ado about Nothing", "Any Questions", "Crossfire"**, etc. But **the Bible** and its books (**Genesis, Ecclesiastes, John,** etc) do not have inverted commas. These rules apply to footnotes as well as bodymatter.

However, book publishers generally use italics for books and pamphlets, plays, radio and television programmes.

3. Lawsuits. If abbreviated, *versus* should always be shortened to *v*, with no point after it. Thus: **Brown** *v* **Board of Education, Coatsworth** *v* **Johnson**.

4. The names of ships, aircraft, spacecraft. Thus: HMS *Illustrious, Spirit of St Louis, Challenger,* etc.
Note that a ship is **she**; a country is **it**.

5. But *The Economist* does not use italics in titles or captions.

J · K

JARGON. Avoid it. All sections of *The Economist* should be intelligible to all our readers, most of whom are foreigners. You may have to think harder if you are not to use jargon, but you can still be precise. Technical terms should be used in their proper context; do not use them out of it. In many instances simple words can do the job of **exponential** (try **fast**), **interface** (**frontier** or **border**), and so on. Avoid, above all, the kind of jargon that tries either to dignify nonsense with seriousness (**Working in an empowering environment**, a topic discussed at a recent Economist conference) or to obscure the truth (**We shall not launch the ground offensive until we have attrited the Republican Guard to the point when they no longer have an effective offensive capacity** – the Pentagon's way of saying that the allies would not fight on the ground until they had killed so many Iraqis that the others would not attack). What was meant by the Israeli defence ministry when it issued the following press release remains unclear: **The United States and Israel now possess the capability to conduct real-time simulations with man in the loop for full-scale theatre missile defence architectures for the Middle East.**

•

KEY: keys may be **major** or **minor**, but not **low**. Few of the decisions, people, industries described as **key** are truly **indispensable**, and fewer still **open locks**.

KNOWLEDGEABLE: verbs are -ableable, but not nouns (with some exceptions such as **profitable**). Try **well informed**.

L

LAG. If you **lag** transitively, you lag a pipe or a loft. Front-runners, rates of growth, fourth-quarter profits and so on are **lagged behind**.

LAST: the last issue of *The Economist* implies our extinction; prefer **last week's** issue, the **previous** issue. Likewise avoid the **last** issue of *Foreign Affairs*: prefer the **latest, current,** or (eg) **June** issue, or **this month's** or **last month's** issue.

    Last year, in 1996, means 1995; if you mean the 12 months up to the time of writing, write **the past year**. The same goes for the **past** month, **past** week, **past** (not **last**) ten years. See also DATES.

LIFESTYLE: prefer **way of life**.

LIGHT-YEAR. A light-year is a measurement of distance, not of time. It is the approximate distance travelled by light in one year.
    Thus: 1 light-year = 5.88×10^{12} miles
                      9.46×10^{12} km

LIKE governs nouns and pronouns, not verbs and clauses. So **as in America** not **like in America**. But **authorities like Fowler and Gowers** is a perfectly acceptable alternative to **authorities such as Fowler and Gowers**.

LOCATE, in all its forms, can usually be replaced by something less ugly. **The missing scientist was located** means he was **found**. **The diplomats will meet at a secret location** means either that they will meet **in a secret place** or that they will meet **secretly**. **A company located in Texas** is simply **a company in Texas**.

LOWER CASE. See CAPITALS.

M

MASTERFUL means **imperious**. **Masterly** means **skilled**.

MAXIMISE means **to make as great as possible. Weight-lifting can maximise your biceps, but not your health.**

MAY and **might** are not always interchangeable, and you may want **may** more often than you think. If in doubt, try **may** first.
You need **might** in the past tense. **I may go to Leeds later** becomes, in the past, **I might have gone to Leeds later.** And in indirect past speech it becomes **I said I might go to Leeds later.**
Conditional sentences using the subjunctive also need **might.** Thus **If I were to go to Leeds, I might have to stand all the way.** This could be rephrased **If I go to Leeds, I may have to stand all the way.** Conditional sentences stating something contrary to fact, however, need **might: If pigs had wings, birds might raise their eyebrows.**
Do not write **Bill Clinton might be president of the United States, but he does not eat broccoli.** It should be **Bill Clinton may be president of the United States, but he does not eat broccoli.** Only if you are putting forward a hypothesis that may or may not be true are **may** and **might** interchangeable. Thus **If Al Gore always eats his broccoli, he may** (or **might**) **become president of the United States.**

MEASUREMENTS. In most contexts that are not American or British, prefer **hectares** to **acres, kilometres** (or **km**) to **miles, metres** to **yards, litres** to **gallons, kilos** to **lb, tonnes** to **tons, Celsius** to **Fahrenheit,** etc. Regardless of which you choose, you should give an equivalent, on first use, in the other units: **It was hoped that after improvements to the engine the car would give 20km to the litre (47 miles per American gallon) compared with its present average of 15km per litre.**
Remember that in few countries do you now buy petrol in imperial gallons. In America it is sold in American gallons; in most places it is sold in litres.
See also MEASURES, page 115ff.

MEDIA: prefer **press and television** or, if the context allows it, just **press.** If you have to use the **media,** remember it is plural.

METAPHORS. "A newly invented metaphor assists thought by evoking a visual image," said George Orwell, "while on the other hand a metaphor which is technically 'dead' (eg, iron resolution) has in effect reverted to being an ordinary word and can generally be used without loss of vividness. But in between these two classes there is a huge dump of wornout metaphors which are merely used because they save people the trouble of inventing phrases for themselves."

Every issue of *The Economist* contains scores of metaphors:

a trail of crushed rivals
billing and cooing politicians
a smaller helping of Europe's
  manifest destiny
a project falling at the first
  hurdle
a weaker grip on monetary
  policy
a track record on inflation
tabloid reporters lapping up
  stories
a report leaving the door ajar
irresistible forces about to
  meet an immovable object
a roadblock in the
  path of reform
investors crying foul
a presidential U-turn
water off a duck's back in the
  Senate
a door slammed shut in China
a blind eye turned in Taiwan

an investor jumping the gun
heat off in America
the reins of power in Japan
a bargaining chip in South
  Africa
a honeymoon (soon to be over)
an iron-clad argument
foot-dragging
a run-up to the election
a counterweight to German
  domination
a shadow cast over the future
bureaucratic barriers
uprooted democracy
grass-roots organisations
mainstream conservatives
young turks
a crash-course in capitalism
grinding poverty
flabby banks getting into shape
politicians turning a deaf ear
a binge of brand acquisitions

Some of these are tired, and will therefore tire the reader. Most are so exhausted that they may be considered dead, and are therefore permissible. But use all metaphors, dead or alive, sparingly, otherwise you will make trouble for yourself.

An issue of *The Economist* chosen at random had a **package cutting the budget deficit, the administration loth to sign on to higher targets, liberals accused of playing politics on the court** (Supreme, not tennis), only to find in the next sentence that **the boot was on the other foot, the lure of eastern Germany as a springboard to the struggling markets of Eastern Europe, West Europeanness helping to dilute an image,** someone **finding a pretext to stall the process** before looking for **a few integrationist crumbs, an end-of-millennium spring clean** that became in the next sentence **a stalking-horse for greater spending,** and **Michelin axing jobs in painful surgery** in order stay at **the top of a league table.** Soon the **Michelin man was plunging his company even further in to debt,** though if it were **to stay afloat his ambitions would have to be deflated.** Little wonder other French firms **were striking out abroad.** The reader had to **go down to the seas again** two pages on when a **flotilla of mutual and quoted life-assurance outfits were confident of surviving turbulent waters. The galleons were afloat,** but **the medium-sized and smaller mutuals** quickly turned into **fodder for domestic and foreign predators.** Further on, **banks going to the altar in the expectation of a tax-free dowry** saw it become a **sweetener** in the next sentence and the bill that delivered it transformed into a **panacea.** Those who wanted to learn about Japanese equity financing were told of a **stockmarket crawling back** (not on its feet, it was explained) **towards its old high,** of **commercial banks keeping the wolf from the door** and, three paragraphs later, **of the stockmarket's double whammy. One whammy was a crash which made a big dent in shares, the other blew a hole (a gaping one) in the so-called** *tokkin* **funds.** On, on went the reader past **masked bunglings, key measures, money-supply growth out of hand, a haunted Bank of Japan redoubling its squeeze, banks slashing**

growth lest they found themselves on a tight leash before being cracked down on. Few could have been surprised to learn at the end of the article that another dose of higher interest rates might be forced on the banks if the present inflationary symptoms turned into measles-like spots, and if the apothecaries at the finance ministry agreed with the diagnosis.

These two sentences, used as an opening paragraph to arrest the attention of the readers of *A.N. Other* newspaper, found their way past its subeditors and into print:

Bulgaria is on its knees. A long-simmering economic crisis has erupted, gripping the country in a fierce and unrelenting embrace.

Another publication lamented:

Mr Clinton has had to pull the plug on a plan that had been tarred as a bail-out for an incompetent regime and the Wall Street fat cats who invested in it.

METE. You may mete out punishment, but if it is to fit the crime it is meet.

MILLIONAIRE: the time has gone when girls in the Bois du Boulogne would think that the term millionaire adequately described the man who broke the Bank at Monte Carlo. If you wish to use it, make it plain that millionaire refers to income (in dollars or pounds), not to capital. Otherwise try plutocrat or rich man.

MINIMISE means to make as small as possible; you cannot slightly minimise something.

MITIGATES mollifies, militates does the opposite.

MONOPOLY. A monopolist is the sole seller; a monopoly buyer is a monopsonist.

MOVE: do not use if you mean decision, bid, deal or something more precise. But move rather than relocate.

N

NAMES

CHINESE NAMES. In general follow the Pinyin spelling, which has replaced the old Wade-Giles system, except for people from the past, and people and places outside mainland China. **Peking** is therefore **Beijing** and **Mao** is **Zedong**, not **Tse-tung**. There are no hyphens in Pinyin spelling. So:

Deng Xiaoping	*But*
Guangdong (Kwangtung)	Chiang Kai-shek
Guangzhou (Canton)	Hong Kong
Hu Yaobang	Li Ka-shing
Jiang Qing (Mrs Mao)	Lee Teng-hui
Mao Zedong (not Tse-tung)	
Qingdao (Tsingtao)	
Tianjin (Tientsin)	
Xinjiang (Sinkiang)	
Zhao Ziyang	

The family name in China comes first, so **Deng Xiaoping** becomes **Mr Deng** on a later mention.

Names from **Singapore, Korea, Vietnam** have no hyphens: **Lee Kuan Yew, Kim Jong Il, Ho Chi Minh**.

See also FOREIGN WORDS AND PHRASES; PEOPLE; TITLES.

DUTCH NAMES. If using first name and surname together, **vans** and **dens** are lower case: **Dries van Agt** and **Joop den Uyl**. But without their first names they become **Mr Van Agt** and **Mr Den Uyl**. This rule does not always apply to Dutch names in Belgium and South Africa; Karel Van Miert, for instance (as well as Mr Van Miert).

FRENCH NAMES: generally follow French convention, capitalising **Le, La, Les, Du** and **Des**, but not **de** or **d'** (unless it starts a sentence).

GERMAN NAMES: von is lower case. But **Otto Habsburg** (no von).

RUSSIAN NAMES. Each of the different approaches to transliterating Russian has its drawbacks. The following rules of thumb are chosen chiefly for reasons of simplicity, not phonetic accuracy.

1. No y before e: **Belarus**, *perestroika*. Exception: if the e starts the word: **Yeltsin, Yevgeny.**

2. Use y before a at the start of a word, but not at the end. **Yavlinsky, Yakovlev, Chechnya** (not **Chechniya**), **Alia** (not **Aliya**). Special case: the president of Turkmenistan is **Saparmurat Niyazov.**

3. Anything pronounced yo is usually spelled e: **Fedorov, Gorbachev.**

4. With words ending -ski, -skii or -sky, choose -sky. But with all other words ending -i, -ii or -y, choose -i. Thus **Zhirinovsky** and **Tchaikovsky**, but **Bolshoi, Nizhni** (Novgorod), **Rutskoi, Yuri.** Exception: **Grigory** (because of the association with Gregory).

5. Replace dzh with j. So: **Jokar (Dudaev), Jaba (Iosseliani).**

NONE usually takes a singular verb. So does **neither** (or **either**) **A nor B**, unless B is plural, as in **Neither the Dutchman nor the Danes have done it**, where the verb agrees with the element closest to it.

NOR means **and not**, so should not be preceded by **and.**

NOT ONLY. This should appear next to the item it qualifies. **His sister loved not only him** and **his sister not only loved him** have different meanings. When used with **but also**, it must either follow the verb or the verb must be repeated, eg, **he not only hurt her feelings but also hurt her pride**, better phrased as **he hurt not only her feelings but also her pride** (see the advice given under BOTH … AND) .

NUMBERS. See FIGURES, MEASUREMENTS, MEASURES (Part III, page 115ff).

O

ONE: try to avoid **one** as a personal pronoun. **You** will often do instead.

ONLY: put **only** as close as you can to the words it qualifies. Thus, **These animals mate only in June.** To say **They only mate in June** implies that in June they do nothing else.

OVERWHELM means **submerge utterly, crush, bring to sudden ruin.** Majority votes, for example, seldom do any of these things. As for the ethnic Albanians in Kosovo, although 90% of the population, they are more likely to be an **overwhelmed majority** rather than an **overwhelming one.**

OXYMORON: an **oxymoron** is not an unintentional contradiction in terms but **a figure of speech in which contradictory terms are deliberately combined,** as in bitter-sweet, cruel kindness, sweet sorrow, etc.

P

PEOPLE. Call them what they want to be called, short of festooning them with titles. Use full stops after initials.
Here are some names which may present problems.

Yasser Arafat
Hafez Assad
Omar el Bashir
Zine El Abidine Ben Ali
Chadli Benjedid
Ritt Bjerregaard
Boutros Boutros-Ghali
Zbigniew Brzezinski
Leopoldo Calvo-Sotelo
Nicolae Ceausescu
Viktor Chernomyrdin
Uncle Tom Cobbleigh
Poul Dalsager
Carlo De Benedetti
Gaston Defferre
Gianni De Michelis
Ciriaco De Mita
Carlo Ripa di Meana
Lawrence Eagleburger
King Fahd
Garret FitzGerald
Yegor Gaidar
Gandhi
Hans-Dietrich Genscher
Felipe Gonzalez
Mikhail Gorbachev
Habsburgs
Elias Hrawi
Saddam Hussein

Ahmad Khomeini
Jeane Kirkpatrick
Slobodan Milosevic
François Mitterrand
Ratko Mladic
Daniel arap Moi
Hosni Mubarak
Muhammad (unless it is part
   of the name of someone who
   spells it differently)
Gaafar Numeiri
Moammar Qaddafi
Ali Akbar Rafsanjani
Edzard Reuter
Nikolai Ryzhkov
Andrei Sakharov
Ali Abdullah Saleh
Wolfgang Schäuble
Yitzhak Shamir
Banharn Silpa-archa
Edward Shevardnadze
George Shultz
Mario Soares (Portugal),
   Adolfo Suarez (Spain)
Alexander Solzhenitsyn
Hans-Jochen Vogel
Caspar Weinberger
Vladimir Zhirinovsky
Gennady Zyuganov

See also FOREIGN WORDS AND PHRASES; NAMES; SPELLING; TITLES.

PER CENT is not the same as a percentage point. Nothing can fall, or be devalued, by more than 100%. If something trebles, it increases by 200%.

PERCOLATE means to pass **through**, not **up** or **down**.

PERSPICACITY and **perspicuity** should be the twin aims of writers: an acuteness of understanding coupled with lucidity of expression.

PHASE: when discussing incomes policies, monetary unions, extended plans, etc, prefer **stage** to **phase**.

PHONE: short but not sweet. Use **telephone**.

PLACES. Use English forms when they are in common use: **Basle, Cologne, Leghorn, Lower Saxony, Lyons, Marseilles, Naples, Nuremberg, Turin.** And English rather than American – **Rockefeller Centre, Pearl Harbour** – unless the place name is part of a company name, such as **Rockefeller Center Properties Inc.** But follow local practice when a country expressly changes its name, or the names of rivers, towns, etc, within it. Thus **Almaty** not **Alma Ata; Chemnitz** not **Karl-Marx-Stadt; Côte d'Ivoire** not **Ivory Coast; Nizhny Novgorod** not **Gorky; Myanmar** not **Burma; Yangon** not **Rangoon;** and **St Petersburg** not **Leningrad.**

Do not use the definite article before **Krajina, Lebanon, Piedmont, Punjab, Sudan, Transkei** and **Ukraine,** but it is **the Caucasus, The Gambia, The Hague, the Maghreb, the Netherlands** – and **La Paz, Le Havre, Los Angeles,** etc. See also COUNTRIES AND THEIR INHABITANTS, and STATES, ETC, page 133.

Do not use the names of capital cities as synonyms for their governments. **Britain will send a gunboat** is fine, but **London will send a gunboat** suggests that this will be the action of the people of London alone. To write **Washington and Moscow now differ only in their approach to Havana** is absurd.

Although the place is **Western** (or **Eastern**) **Europe,** the people are **West** or **East Europeans.**

Here are the spellings of some common problematic place names.

Abkhazia
Argentina (adj and
  people Argentine,
  not Argentinian)
Ashgabat
Azerbaijan
Baden-Württemberg
Baghdad
Bahrain
Bangladesh
Basle
Belarus
Bophuthatswana

Bosporus
Cameroon
Cape Town
Caribbean
Cincinnati
Colombia (South
  America)
Columbia (university, District of);
  British Columbia
Cracow
Dar es Salaam
Djibouti

Dominica
  (Caribbean island)
Dominican Republic
  (part of another
  island)
El Salvador,
  Salvadorean
Gettysburg
Gothenburg
Grozny
Gujarat, Gujarati
Guyana (*but* French
  Guiana)

Hanover	Macau	Salzburg
Harare	Mauritania	St Petersburg
Hercegovina	Middlesbrough	Sebastopol
Hong Kong (but one	Nagorno-Karabakh	Sindh
word in Hongkong	North Rhine-	Srebrenica
and Shanghai Banking	Westphalia	Sri Lanka
Corporation)	Nuremberg	Strasbourg
Issyk-Kul	Philippines (the	Suriname
Jeddah	people are Filipinos	Taipei
KaNgwane	and Filipinas)	Tajikistan
Katmandu	Phnom Penh	Teesside
Kazakhstan	Pittsburgh	Tehran
Kirgizstan	Pyrenean	Tigray, Tigrayan
Kuwait city	Quezon City	Transdniestria
KwaNdebele	Reykjavik	Uzbekistan
KwaZulu-Natal	Romania	Valletta
Luhansk	Salonika (not	Yugoslavia
Luxembourg	Thessaloniki)	Zepce

PLANE: this is a **tool**, a **surface** or sometimes, if it flies, it is an **aeroplane**, **aircraft** or **airliner** (not an **airplane**). **Warplane**, however, is allowed.

PLANTS: see ANIMALS, PLANTS, ETC.

PLURALS. No rules here. The spelling of the following plurals may be decided by either practice or derivation.

-oes

archipelagoes	haloes	potatoes
buffaloes	heroes	salvoes
cargoes	innuendoes	tomatoes
desperadoes	mementoes	tornadoes
echoes	mosquitoes	torpedoes
embargoes	mottoes	vetoes
grottoes	noes	volcanoes

-os

altos	ghettos	quangos
commandos	impresarios	radios
concertos	librettos	silos
contraltos	manifestos	solos
dynamos	mulattos	sopranos
embryos	oratorios	stilettos
Eskimos	peccadillos	studios
fiascos	pianos	virtuosos
folios	provisos	

-ums

conundrums	moratoriums	stadiums
crematoriums	nostrums	symposiums
curriculums	quorums	ultimatums
forums	referendums	vacuums

-a

addenda	criteria	the spirit world)
bacteria	data	memoranda
consortia	errata	phenomena
corpora (plural of	genera (plural of	quanta
corpus)	genus)	sanatoria
corrigenda	media (but mediums	spectra
crematoria	communicate with	strata

-uses

caucuses	fetuses	geniuses
circuses	focuses	prospectuses

-i

alumni	fungi	stimuli
bacilli	graffiti	termini
cacti	nuclei	

-s

agendas	milieus	plateaus
arenas	panaceas	quotas

-ae

amoebae	lacunae	vertebrae
formulae	nebulae	

-ves   **-fs**

calves	dwarfs
hooves	handkerchiefs
scarves	roofs
wharves	turfs

-eaus   **-eaux**

bureaus(*but* bureaux de change)   chateaux
tableaus

-es

amanuenses	bases	oases
analyses	crises	synopses
antitheses	hypotheses	

Note: indexes (of books); indices are indicators of index numbers; appendixes (anatomical variety; use appendices for literary sort).

PRECIPITOUS means **extremely steep**; a rash or hasty action is **precipitate**. **Precipitate share dealings led to a precipitous drop in prices.**

PREPOSITIONS at the end of sentences are permissible: **an example such as this is a good one to go by**, rather than **an example such as this is a good one by which to go.**

PRESENTLY means **soon**, not **at present**. **"Presently Kep opened the door of the shed, and let out Jemima Puddle-Duck."**

PREVARICATE means **evade the truth**; **procrastinate** means **delay.**

PRISTINE means **original** or **former condition**, not **pure** or **clean.**

PROBLEM: the problem with problem is it is overused, so much so that it is becoming a problem word.

PROOF-READING

Look for errors in the following categories.

1. "Typos", which include misspelt words, punctuation mistakes, wrong numbers, transposed words or sentences.
2. Bad word breaks (see below).
3. Layout mistakes: wrongly positioned text (including captions, headings, folios, running heads) or illustrations, incorrect line spacing, missing items, widows (short lines at the top of a page).
4. Wrong fonts: errors in the use of italic, bold, etc.

Additionally, if the text contains cross-references to numbered pages or illustrations, the proof-reader is usually responsible for inserting the correct reference at page proof stage, and for checking cross-references.

The most effective way of proof-reading is to read the text several times, each time with a different focus, rather than attempting to carry out all checks in one go. This helps concentration and makes it easier to detect inconsistencies which are usually the sign of an error.

WORD BREAKS. If text is justified, or contains many long words, it may be necessary to break words, using a hyphen, at the end of lines. The aim should be to make these breaks as undisruptive as possible, so that the reader does not stumble or falter. Whenever possible, the word should be broken so that, helped by the context, the reader can anticipate the whole word from the part of it given before the break. Here are some useful principles for deciding how to break a word.

1. Words that are already hyphenated should be broken at the hyphen, not given a second hyphen.
2. Words can be broken according to either their derivation (the British convention) or their pronunciation (the US convention): thus, **aristo-cracy** (UK) or **aristoc-racy** (US), **melli-fluous** (UK) or **mellif-luous** (US). See PART II for American usage.
3. Words of one syllable should not be broken.
4. Words of five or fewer characters should not be broken.
5. At least three characters must be taken over to the next line.
6. Words should not be broken so that their identity is confused or their identifying sound is distorted: thus, avoid **wo-men,** or **fo-ist**.
7. Personal names should not be broken.
8. Figures should not be broken or separated from their unit of measurement.
9. A word formed with a prefix or suffix should be broken at that point: thus, **bi-furcated, ante-diluvian, convert-ible**.
10. If a breakable word contains a double consonant, split it at that point: thus, **as-sess, ship-ping, prob-lem**.

PROOF-READING MARKS. Proof-reading marks are illustrated on the following pages, though some people use different ones for certain things. The intention of these marks is to identify, precisely and concisely, the nature of an error and, when necessary, the correction required. When corrections are extensive or complex, it is usually better to spell out, in full, the correct form of the text rather than leave the typesetter to puzzle over a string of hieroglyphs, however immaculately drawn and ordered. Be careful, though, to use capital letters and lower case as appropriate; mark all proof corrections clearly, keeping all letters separate, and write them in the margin in the order in which they fall on the line.

Instruction	Textual mark	Marginal mark & notes
Correction is concluded	None	Make after each correction
Leave unchanged	.... under characters to remain	stet
Remove extraneous marks	Encircle marks to be removed	eg, film or paper edges visible between lines on bromide proofs
Push down risen spacing material	Encircle blemish	
Refer to appropriate authority anything of doubtful accuracy	Encircle word(s) affected	
Insert in text the matter indicated in the margin	(caret mark)	New matter followed by
Insert additional matter identified by a letter in a diamond		Followed by for example Ⓐ	The relevant section of the copy should be supplied with the corresponding letter marked on it in a diamond, eg Ⓐ
Delete	/ through character(s) or ⊢——⊣ through words to be deleted	
Delete and close up	through character(s) or through characters, eg, charaacter, charaaacter	

Instruction	Textual mark	Marginal mark & notes
Close up – delete space	⌒	⌒
Substitute character or substitute part of one or more word(s)	through character / or through words	new character or new word(s)
Wrong font Replace by characters of correct font	Encircle character(s) to be changed	⊗ or w.f.
Correct damaged character(s)	Encircle character(s) to be changed	✕
Set in or change to roman type	Encircle character(s) to be changed	Rom.
Set in or change to italic	under character(s) to to be set or changed	ital.
Set in or change to capital letters	under character(s) to be set or changed	≡ or caps.
Set in or change to small capital letters	under character(s) to be set or changed	= or s.c.
Set in or change to capital letters for initial letters and small capital letters for the rest of the words	under initial letters under rest of word(s)	
Set in or change to bold type	under character(s) to be set or changed	or bold
Set in or change to bold italic type	under character(s) to be set or changed	
Change capital letters to lower case letters	Encircle character(s) to be changed	≢ or l.c.

Instruction	Textual mark	Marginal mark & notes
Invert type	Encircle character to be changed	↻
Substitute or insert character in "superior" position	/ through character or ⋀ where required	⋎ under character e.g. ²⋎
Substitute or insert character in "inferior" position	/ through character or ⋀ where required	⋏ over character e.g. ⋏2
Substitute ligature e.g. ffi for separate letters	through characters affected	⌒ ⌒ ⌣ e.g. **ffi**
Substitute separate letters for ligature		Write out separate letters
Substitute or insert full stop or decimal point	/ through character or ⋀ where required	⊙/
Substitute or insert colon	/ through character or ⋀ where required	⊙/
Substitute or insert semi-colon	/ through character or ⋀ where required	;
Insert space	⋏	# ⋏
Equal space	‖ between words or letters	equal # /
Reduce space	‖ between words or letters	less # /

Instruction	Textual mark	Marginal mark & notes
Substitute or insert oblique	/ through character or ∧ where required	(encircled oblique)
Start new paragraph	[	n.p.
Run on (no new paragraph)	⌣	⌣
Transpose characters or words	(transpose mark) between characters or words, numbered when necessary	(transpose mark) and/or trs.
Transpose a number of characters or words	3 2 1 | | |	1 2 3 The vertical strokes are made through the characters or words to be transposed and numbered in the correct sequence
Transpose lines	(S-shaped mark)	(S-shaped mark)
Transpose a number of lines	———————3 ———————2 ———————1	Rules extend from the margin into the text with each line to be transplanted numbered in the correct sequence
Centre	⌈enclosing matter to be centred⌉	[ ]
Indent or move to the right	(indent mark)	(indent mark) Give the amount of the indent in the marginal mark
Move to the left	(move left mark)	(move left mark) Give the amount of the indent in the marginal mark
Abbreviation or figure to be spelt out in full	Encircle matter to be altered	(spell out)
Insert single or double quotes	∧ ∧	' ' " "

PROPAGANDA (which is singular) means **a systematic effort to spread doctrine or opinions**. It is not a synonym for **lies**.

PROPER NOUNS: if they have adjectives, use them. Thus a **Californian** (not **California**) **judge**, the **Pakistani** (not **Pakistan**) **government**, the **Texan** (not **Texas**) **press**.

PROTEST. Objectors protest that a decision is unfair, or they protest at or against it. **Employers have protested against the examination boards' decision to take no account of spelling in A-level marking systems** is right; **The** NUT **protested the penalisation of children from ethnic minorities for writing poor English** is wrong.

PRY: use **prise**, unless you mean **peer**.

PUNCTUATION

APOSTROPHES. Use the normal possessive ending **'s** after singular words or names that end in **s: boss's, caucus's, Delors's, St James's, Jones's, Shanks's**. Use it after plurals that do not end in **s: children's, Frenchmen's, media's**.

Use the ending **s'** on plurals that end in **s** – **Danes', bosses', Joneses'** – including plural names that take a singular verb, eg, **Reuters', Barclays', Stewarts & Lloyds', Salomon Brothers'**.

Although singular in other respects, the United States, the United Nations, the Philippines, etc, have a plural possessive apostrophe: eg, **What will the United States' next move be? Peoples'** = of peoples.
People's = of (the) people.

Try to avoid using **Lloyd's** (the insurance market) as a possessive; it poses an insoluble problem.

Do not put apostrophes into decades: the **1990s** not the **1990's**.

BRACKETS. If a whole sentence is within brackets, put the full stop inside.

Square brackets should be used for interpolations in direct quotations: **"Let them [the poor] eat cake."** To use ordinary curved brackets implies that the words inside them were part of the original.

COLONS. Use a colon "to deliver the goods that have been invoiced in the preceding words" (Fowler). **They brought presents: gold, frankincense and oil at $35 a barrel.**

Use a colon before a whole quoted sentence, but not before a quotation that begins mid-sentence. **She said: "It will never work." He retorted that it had "always worked before".**

Use a colon for antithesis or "gnomic contrasts" (Fowler). **Man proposes: God disposes.**

COMMAS. Use commas as an aid to understanding. Too many in one sentence can be confusing.

It is not necessary to put a comma after a short phrase at the start of a sentence if no natural pause exists there: **On August 2nd he invaded. Next time the world will be prepared.** But a breath, and so a comma, is needed after longer passages: **When it was plain that he had his eyes on Saudi Arabia as well as Kuwait, America responded.**

Use two commas, or none at all, when inserting a clause in the middle of a sentence. Thus, do not write: **Use two commas, or none at all when inserting** ... or **Use two commas or none at all, when inserting** ...

If the clause ends with a bracket, which is not uncommon (this one does), the bracket should be followed by a comma.

Do not put a comma before **and** at the end of a sequence of items unless one of the items includes another **and**. Thus **The doctor suggested an aspirin, half a grapefruit and a cup of broth.** But **He ordered scrambled eggs, whisky and soda, and a selection from the trolley.** But American usage is different; see PART II.

Commas can alter the sense of a sentence. To write **Mozart's 40th symphony, in G minor**, with commas indicates that this symphony was written in G minor. Without commas, **Mozart's 40th symphony in G minor** suggests he wrote 39 other symphonies in G minor.

Commas in dates: none.

Do not put commas after question marks, even when they would be separated by quotation marks: **"May I have a second helping?" he asked.**

DASHES. You can use dashes in pairs for parenthesis, but not more than one pair per sentence, ideally not more than one pair per paragraph. (See also HYPHENS.)

Use a dash to introduce an explanation, amplification, paraphrase, particularisation or correction of what immediately precedes it.

Use it to gather up the subject of a long sentence.

Use it to introduce a paradoxical or whimsical ending to sentences.

Do not use the dash as a punctuation maid-of-all-work (Gower).

FULL STOPS. Use plenty. They keep sentences short. This helps the reader.

Do not use full stops in ABBREVIATIONS or at the end of headings.

INVERTED COMMAS (QUOTATION MARKS). Use single ones only

for quotations within quotations. Thus: **"When I say 'immediately', I mean some time before April," said the spokesman.**

When a quotation is indented and set in smaller type than the main bodymatter, do not put inverted commas around it.

For the relative placing of quotation marks and punctuation, follow Hart's rules. If an extract ends with a full stop or question-mark, put the punctuation before the closing inverted commas. **His maxim was that "love follows laughter." In this spirit came his opening gambit: "What's the difference between a buffalo and a bison?"** If a complete sentence in quotes comes at the end of a longer sentence, the final stop should be inside the inverted commas. Thus, **The answer was, "You can't wash your hands in a buffalo." She replied, "Your jokes are execrable."**

If the quotation does not include any punctuation, the closing inverted commas should precede any punctuation marks that the sentence requires. Thus: **She had already noticed that the "young man" looked about as young as the New Testament is new. Although he had been described as "fawnlike in his energy and playfulness", "a stripling with all the vigour and freshness of youth", and even as "every woman's dream toyboy", he struck his companion-to-be as the kind of old man warned of by her mother as "not safe in taxis". Where, now that she needed him, was "Mr Right"?**

When a quotation is broken off and resumed after such words as **he said**, ask yourself whether it would naturally have had any punctuation at the point where it is broken off. If the answer is yes, a comma is placed within the quotation marks to represent this. Thus, **"If you'll let me see you home," he said, "I think I know where we can find a cab."** The comma after **home** belongs to the quotation and so comes within the inverted commas, as does the final full stop.

But if the words to be quoted are continuous, without punctuation at the point where they are broken, the comma should be outside the inverted commas. Thus, **"My bicycle", she assured him, "awaits me."**

See PART II, pages 85–86, for American usage.

QUESTION-MARKS. Except in sentences that include a question in inverted commas, question-marks always come at the end of the sentence. Thus: **Where could he get a drink, he wondered?**

SEMI-COLONS. Semi-colons should be used to mark a pause longer than a comma and shorter than a full stop. Don't overdo them.

Use them to distinguish phrases listed after a colon if commas will not do the job clearly. Thus, **They agreed on only three points: the ceasefire should be immediate; it should be internationally supervised, preferably by the OAU; and a peace conference should be held, either in Geneva or in Ouagadougou.**

R

RACISM. As a general rule, a person's race, colour or creed should be mentioned only when relevant. See ETHNIC GROUPS.

REAL. Is it really necessary? When used to mean **after taking inflation into account,** it is legitimate. In other contexts (**Investors are showing real interest in the country, but Bolivians wonder if real prosperity will ever arrive**), it is often better left out.

REBUT and **refute** mean **to put to flight,** or disprove, in argument. They are not synonyms for **deny.** ("**Shakespeare never has six lines together without a fault. Perhaps you may find seven: but this does not refute my general assertion.**" Samuel Johnson)

REGRETTABLY means it is to be regretted that; someone who shows regret is behaving **regretfully. It is regrettably true that few people respond regretfully when told they have dropped some litter.**

RELATIONSHIP is a long word often better replaced by **relations. The two countries hope for a better relationship** means **The two countries hope for better relations.**

RELATIVE: fine as an adjective, but as a noun prefer **relation.**

REPORT on, not **into.**

S

SAME. often superfluous. If your sentence contains **on the same day that**, try **on the day that**.

SCOTCH: to **scotch** means to **disable**, not to **destroy**. ("**We have scotched the snake, not killed it**"). The people may be Scots or Scottish (whisky is **Scotch**); choose as you like. **Scot-free** means **free from payment of a fine** (or **punishment**), not free from Scotsmen.

SECTOR: try **industry** instead or, for example, **banks** instead of **banking sector**.

SEQUESTERED means **secluded**. **Sequestrated** means **confiscated**.

SEXISM. It is often possible to phrase sentences so that they neither give offence to women nor become hideously complicated. Using the plural can be helpful. Thus **Instruct the reader without lecturing him** is better put as **Instruct the readers without lecturing them.** But some sentences cannot be satisfactorily rephrased in the plural: **Find a good teacher and take his advice** is not easily rendered gender-neutral. Avoid, above all, the sort of scrambled syntax that the Commission for Racial Equality had to adopt because it could not bring itself to use a singular pronoun: **We can't afford to squander anyone's talents, whatever colour their skin is.**

Avoid **chairperson** (chairwoman is permissible), **humankind** and **person in the street** – ugly expressions all. But remember that, in some contexts, the assumption that all people are men will be especially annoying just because it is wrong. **He will have to choose the best man for the job** is fine if you are talking about the pope selecting a bishop. If you are talking about John Major appointing a new member of cabinet, it would be better to say **He will have to choose the best person for the job.**

Do not use words that make unwarranted assumptions about the sex of an interest group. Do you mean **housewives** or **consumers**, **mothers** or **parents**?

Refer to **women**, not **girls** (unless they are under 18) or **ladies**. **If more women read** *The Economist*, **there would be fewer jobs for the boys.**

SHORT WORDS. Use them. They are often Anglo-Saxon rather than Latin in origin. They are easy to spell and easy to understand. Thus prefer **about** to **approximately**, **after** to **following**, **let** to **permit**, **but** to **however**, **use** to **utilise**, **make** to **manufacture**, **plant** to **facility**, **take part** to **participate**, **set up** to **establish**, **enough** to **sufficient**, **show** to **demonstrate**, and so on. **Under-developed** countries are often better described as **poor**. **Substantive** usually means **real** or **big**.

SIMPLISTIC: prefer **simple-minded, naive**.

SLANG. Do not be too free with **slang** (eg, **He really hit the big time in 1995**). Slang, like metaphors, should be used only occasionally if it is to have effect. Avoid expressions used only by journalists, such as giving people **the thumbs up, the thumbs down** or **the green light**. Stay clear of **gravy trains** and **salami tactics**. Do not use **the likes of**. And avoid words or expressions that are ugly or overused, such as **the bottom line, caring** (as an adjective), **carers, guesstimate** (use **guess**), **schizophrenic** (unless the context is medical), **crisis, key, major** (unless something else nearby is **minor**), **massive** (as in **massive inflation**), **meaningful, perceptions** and **prestigious**.

Politicians are often said to be highly **visible**, when **conspicuous** would be more appropriate. Regulations are sometimes said to be designed to create **transparency**, which presumably means openness.

Try not to be predictable, especially not predictably jocular. Spare your readers any mention of **mandarins** when writing about the civil service, of **their lordships** when discussing the House of Lords, and of **comrades** when analysing communist parties.

SMALL CAPITALS. Use SMALL CAPITALS for most abbreviations consisting of the first letter(s) of the abbreviated word(s). Exceptions are: currencies; degrees of temperature; some measures; Latin words. See also ABBREVIATIONS.

SOME TIME means **at some point**; **sometime** means **former**.

SPELLING

Use British English rather than American English or any other kind (see also PART II). Sometimes, however, this injunction will clash with the rule that people and companies should be called what they want to be called, short of festooning themselves with titles. If it does, adopt American (or Canadian or other local) spelling when it is used in the name of an American (etc) company or private organisation (**Alcan Aluminum, Pulverizing Services Inc, Travelers Insurance**), but not when it is used for a place or government institution (**Pearl**

Harbour, Department of Defence, Department of Labour). The principle behind this ruling is that place names are habitually changed from foreign languages into English: **Deutschland** becomes **Germany, München Munich, Torino Turin**, etc. And to respect the local spelling of government institutions would present difficulties: a sentence containing both the **Department of Labor** and the **secretary of labour**, or the **Defense Department** and the **need for a strong defence**, would look unduly odd. That oddity will arise nonetheless if you have to explain that **Rockefeller Center Properties is in charge of Rockefeller Centre**, but with luck that will not happen too often.

The Australian **Labor Party** should be spelt without a **u** not only because it is not a government institution but also because the Australians spell it that way, although they spell **labour** as the British do.

Use **-ise, -isation** (**realise, organisation**) throughout. But please do not **hospitalise**.

Follow the preferences of companies or individuals themselves in writing their names.

For spelling rules for place names, see CITIES; COUNTRIES AND THEIR INHABITANTS; NAMES; PLACES; STATES, REGIONS, PROVINCES, COUNTIES.

For spelling rules for other proper names, see PEOPLE and COMPANIES. Other common difficulties are listed below (and see also -ABLE, -EABLE, -IBLE. See also PART II for American spellings.

Common problems

abattoir
accommodate
acknowledgment
acquittal
adviser, advisory
aeroplane, aircraft, airliner
aesthetic
Afrikaans (the language),
  Afrikaner (the person)
ageing (*but* caging, paging,
  raging, waging)
ambience
amid (*not* amidst)
amok (*not* amuck)
annex (verb), annexe (noun)
appal, appals, appalling,
  appalled
aqueduct
aquifer
arbitrager
artefact

asinine
balk (*not* baulk)
balloted, balloting
bandwagon
battalion
benefited
biased
bicentenary (noun, *not*
  bicentennial)
billeted
blanketing
block (*never* bloc)
bogey (bogie is on a locomotive)
born (given birth to),
  borne (carried)
borsch
braggadocio
brethren
bused, busing (keep bussing
  for kissing)
by-election, bypass, by-product

bye (in sport only)
bye-law (different root from by-election, etc)
cannon (gun), canon (standard, criterion, clergyman)
canvas (cloth), canvass (seek opinion), canvassed
carcass
caviare
chancy
channelled
chaperon
checking account (spell it thus when explaining to Americans a current account, which is to be preferred)
choosy
cipher
clubable
combating
commemorate
complement (make complete), compliment (praise)
connection
consensus
cooled, cooly
coral (stuff found in sea), corral (cattle pen)
coruscate
cosseted
council (assembly)
counsel (give advice)
counsellor
defendant
dependant (person) dependent (adj)
depository (*unless* referring to American depositary receipts)
desiccation
detente (*not* détente)
dexterous (*not* dextrous)
discreet (prudent), discrete (separate)
disk (in a computer context), *otherwise* disc
dispatch (*not* despatch)
dispel, dispelling

dissect
dissociate (*not* disassociate)
distil, distiller
divergences
douse (drench), dowse (use a divining rod)
dwelt
dyeing (colour)
dyke
ecstasy
embarrass (*but* harass)
encyclopedia
enroll, enrolment
ensure (make certain), insure (against risks)
enthrall
farther (distance), further (additional)
favour, favourable
ferreted
fetid
fetus (*not* foetus, misformed from the Latin *fetus*)
Filipino, Filipina (person), Philippine (adj of the Philippines)
filleted
flier, high-flier
flotation
focused, focusing
forbear (abstain), forebear (ancestor)
forbid (past tense forbade)
foreboding
foreclose
forefather
forestall
forewarn
forgather
forgo (do without), forego (precede)
forsake
forswear, forsworn
for ever (for all time), forever (unceasingly)
fuelled
-ful, *not* -full (armful,

bathful, handful, etc)
fulfil, fulfilling
fullness
fulsome
gauge
glamour
gram (*not* gramme)
grey
grill (cook under flame)
grille (grating)
grisly (gruesome),
  grizzly (grey-haired;
  kind of bear)
guerrilla
gypsy
haemorrhage,
  haemorrhoids
hallo (*not* hello)
harass (*but* embarrass)
hiccup (*not* hiccough)
high-tech
hotch-potch
hurrah (*not* hooray)
hypocrisy, hypocrite
idiosyncrasy
idyll
impresario
inadvertent
incur, incurring
innocuous
inoculate
inquire, inquiry (*not* enquire,
  enquiry)
install, instalment, installation
instil, instilling
intransigent
jail (*not* gaol)
jewellery (*not* jewelry)
judgment
labelled
lacquer
laisser-faire
lama (priest), llama (beast)
lambast
leukaemia
levelled
liaise

libelled
licence (noun), license (verb)
lightening (making light),
  lightning (thunder and)
limited
linchpin, *but* lynch law
liquefy
liqueur (flavoured alcoholic
  drink)
liquor (alcohol or other liquid)
literal (exact, factual, etc),
  littoral (shore)
loth (reluctant),
  loath (hate), loathsome
low-tech
manoeuvre (manoeuvring)
mantelpiece
marshal (noun and verb)
marshalled
mayonnaise
medieval
mêlée
meter (instrument for
  measuring),
  metre (linear measurement)
mileage
millennium (thousand years)
minuscule
modelled
mould
mouth (noun and verb)
mujahiddin
Muslim (*not* Moslem)
naivety
'Ndrangheta
nonplussed
nought (for numerals),
  otherwise naught
obbligato
occur, occurring
optics (optician)
paediatric (-ian)
panel, panelled
parallel (-ed)
  paralleling
pastime
pavilion

pedal (noun and verb,
  relating to foot lever)
peddle (to deal in trifles), *but*
  pedlar (not peddler)
peninsula (noun),
  peninsular (adj)
phoney (*not* phony)
piggyback (*not* pickaback)
plummeted
practice (noun), practise (verb)
predilection
preferred (-ing, *but* proffered)
preventive (*not* preventative)
principal (head; loan; or adj),
  principle (abstract noun)
privilege
proffered (-ing, *but* preferred)
profited
program (only in a computer
  context *otherwise* programme)
pronunciation
protester
pygmy
pzazz
questionnaire
queuing
rack (-ed, -ing, as in with pain,
  nerve-racking)
racket
rankle
rarefy
raze (*not* rase)
razzmattazz
recur, recurrent, recurring
refrigerator (*but* fridge)
regretted
renege
repairable (able to be repaired),
  reparable (of loss, able to be
  made good)
resemble, resemblance
restaurant
restaurateur
resuscitate
rococo
rottweiler
saccharin (noun),

saccharine (adj)
sacrilegious
salutary (remedial),
  salutatory (welcoming)
sanatorium
savannah
sceptic
seize
shaky
sheath (noun), sheathe (verb)
shibboleth
siege
sieve
skulduggery
smelt
smidgen (*not* smidgeon)
smoky
smooth (both noun and verb)
soothe
souped up
soyabean
specialty (*only* in context of
  medicine, steel and chemicals),
  otherwise speciality
sphinx
spoilt
stationary (adj, not moving
  or movable)
stationery (noun, writing
  paper, etc)
storey (floor)
straight (without curves)
straits (narrow passage of water;
  position of difficulty)
straitjacket
straitlaced
stratagem
strategy
supersede
swap (*not* swop)
synonym
tariff
teetotalism, teetotaller
threshold
titbits
titillate
tormentor

trade union, trade unions
 (*but* Trades Union Congress)
transatlantic (*unless* trans-Pacific
 occurs close to it, when it must
 be trans-Atlantic)
transferred (-ing)
transsexual
travelled
tricolour
trouper (as in old trouper)
unparalleled
untrammelled

vaccinate
vacillate
visor
wagon (*not* waggon)
waive (to relinquish rights)
waver (to vacillate, tremble)
whisky (Scotch), whiskey (Irish)
wilful
withhold
wreath (noun),
 wreathe (verb)
wry, wrily

SPECIFIC: a **specific** is a **medicine**, not a detail.

SPLIT INFINITIVES. To never split an infinitive is quite easy.

STATIONARY: still. **Stationery**: writing paper and so on.

STRAIGHT means **direct** or **uncurved**; **strait** means **narrow** or **tight**. The **strait-laced** tend to be **straight-faced**.

-STYLE: avoid **German-style supervisory boards, an** EC-**style rotating presidency,** etc. Explain what you mean.

SUBCONTRACT. If you engage someone to do something, you are **contracting** the job to him; only if he then asks someone else to do it is the job **subcontracted**.

SUBJUNCTIVES. See INTRODUCTION, pages 6–7; MAY AND MIGHT.

T

TABLE: avoid it as a transitive verb. In Britain to **table** means to bring something forward for action. In America it means the opposite.

TARGET is a noun. If you are tempted to use it as a verb, try **aim** or **direct. Targeted** means **provided with a shield.**

THERE IS, THERE ARE: often unnecessary. **There were smiles on every face** is better as **A smile was on every face. There are three issues facing the prime minister** is better as **Three issues face the prime minister.**

TIMES: take care. **Three times more than x** means **four times as much as x.**

TITLES.
The overriding principle is to treat people with respect. That usually means giving them the title they themselves adopt. But some titles are misleading (all Italian graduates are Dr), and some tiresomely long (Mr Dr Dr Federal Sanitary-Inspector Schmidt). Do not indulge people's self-importance unless it would seem insulting not to.

Do not use Mr, Mrs, Miss, Ms or Dr on first mention even in bodymatter. Plain Bill Clinton, John Major or other appropriate combination of first name and surname will do. But thereafter the names of all living people should be preceded by Mr, Mrs, Ms, Miss or some other title. Knights, dames, lords, princes, kings, etc, should be given their title on first and subsequent mentions.

Titles are not necessary in headings or captions (surnames are; no Johns, Bills, etc). Sometimes they can also be dispensed with for athletes and rock stars, if titles would make them seem more

ridiculous than dignified, and for criminals whose misdeeds are egregious. No titles for the dead, except those whom you are writing about because they have just died. **Dr Johnson** and **Mr Gladstone** are also permissible.

Take care with foreign titles. Malaysian ones are so confusing that it is wise to dispense with them altogether. Do not, however, call **Tunku Razaleigh Hamzah** Mr Razaleigh Hamzah; if you are not giving him his Tunku, refer to him, on each mention, as **Razaleigh Hamzah**. Avoid, above all, Mr Tunku Razaleigh Hamzah.

Use **Dr** only for qualified medical people, unless the correct alternative is not known or it would seem perverse to use **Mr**. And try to keep **Professor** for those who hold chairs, not just a university job or inflated ego.

If you use a title, get it right. **Rear-Admiral** Jones should not, at least on first mention, be called **Admiral** Jones.

Governor X, President Y, the Rev John Z may be **Mr, Mrs** or **Miss** on second mention.

Life peeresses should be called **Lady**, not **Baroness**, just as barons are called **Lord**.

On first mention use forename and surname; thereafter drop forename (unless there are two people with the same surname mentioned in the article). **Jacques Chirac** then **Mr Chirac**.

Avoid nicknames and diminutives unless the person is always known (or prefers to be known) by one: **Bill Emmott, Tony Blair, Tiny Rowland, Bill Clinton, Newt Gingrich**.

Avoid the habit of joining office and name: **Prime Minister Major, Budget Commissioner Liikanen**, but **Chancellor Kohl** is permissible.

Omit middle initials. Nobody will imagine that the **Lyndon Johnson** you are writing about is **Lyndon A. Johnson** or **Lyndon C. Johnson**.

The title **Ms**, created to provide a female equivalent for the all-purpose male title **Mr**, is permissible though ugly. Married women who are known by their maiden names – eg, Aung San Suu Kyi, Benazir Bhutto, Jane Fonda – are **Miss** unless they have made it clear that they want to be called something else. Whenever possible, find out which title the woman herself prefers.

Some titles serve as names, and therefore have initial capitals, though they also serve as descriptions: **the Archbishop of Canterbury, the Emir of Kuwait**. If you want to describe the office rather than the individual, use lower case: **The next archbishop of Canterbury will be a woman**. Use lower case, too, in references simply to **the archbishop, the emir, the shah: The Duchess of Scunthorpe was in her finery, but the duke wore jeans**.

TOTAL: all right as a noun, but as a verb prefer **amount to** or **add up to**.

U

UNIQUE means **the only one of its kind** and cannot be qualified; it is nonsense to describe something **almost/rather/the most unique**.

UNLIKE should not be followed by **in**.

UNNECESSARY WORDS. Some words add nothing but length to your prose. Use adjectives to make your meaning more precise and be cautious of those you find yourself using to make it more emphatic. The word **very** is a case in point. If it occurs in a sentence you have written, try leaving it out. **The omens were good** may have more force than **The omens were very good**.

Avoid **strike action** (**strike** will do), **cutbacks** (**cuts**), **track record** (**record**), **wilderness area** (usually either a **wilderness** or a **wild area**), **large-scale** (**big**), **weather conditions** (**weather**), etc.

Shoot off, or rather shoot, as many prepositions after verbs as possible. Thus people can **meet** rather than **meet with**; companies can be **bought** and **sold** rather than **bought up** and **sold off**; budgets can be **cut** rather than **cut back**; plots can be **hatched** but not **hatched up**; organisations should be **headed** by rather than **headed up** by chairmen just as markets should be **freed**, rather than **freed up**. And children can be **sent** to bed rather than **sent off** to bed.

The word **community** is usually unnecessary. So the **black community** means **blacks**, the **business community** means **business**, the **homosexual community** means **homosexuals**, the **international community**, if it means anything, means **other countries**, **aid agencies** or, just occasionally, **the family of nations**.

Use words with care. A **heart condition** is usually a **bad heart**. **Positive thoughts** presumably means **optimism**, just as a **negative report** is probably a **critical report**. **Industrial action** is usually **industrial inaction, industrial disruption** or **strike**. A **substantially finished** bridge is an **unfinished** bridge, a **major speech** usually just a **speech**. Something with **reliability problems** probably **does not work**. If yours is a **live audience**, what would a dead one be like?

USE AND ABUSE: two words much used and abused. You **take** drugs, not **use** them (Does he use sugar?). And **drug abuse** is just **drug taking**, as is **substance abuse**, unless it is **glue sniffing** or **bun throwing**.

V · W

VENAL. In some countries, petty officials are **venal** – that is, open to bribery. But, when you consider how little they are paid, you may count it a **venial** – that is, pardonable – sin.

VENERABLE means **worthy of reverence**. It is not a synonym for **old**.

VENUES: avoid them. Try **places**.

VERBAL: every agreement, except the nod-and-wink variety, is **verbal**. If you mean one that was not written down, describe it as **oral**.

VIABLE means **capable of living**. Do not apply it to things like railway lines. **Economically viable** means **profitable**.

•

WARN is transitive, so you must either **give warning** or **warn somebody**.

WHICH informs, **that** defines. **This is the house that Jack built.** But **This house, which Jack built, is now falling down.**

WHILE is best used temporally. Do not use it in place of **although** or **whereas**.

PART II

AMERICAN AND BRITISH ENGLISH

The differences between English as written and spoken in America and English as used in Britain are considerable, as is the potential for misunderstanding, even offence, when using words or phrases that are unfamiliar or mean something else on the other side of the Atlantic. This section highlights the important differences of American and British English spelling, grammar and usage.

VOCABULARY. Sometimes the same word has taken on different meanings on the two sides of the Atlantic, creating an opportunity for misunderstanding. The word **homely**, for example, means **simple** or **informal** in British English, but **plain** or **unattractive** in American English.

This also applies to figures of speech. **It went like a bomb** in British English means it was a great success; **it bombed** in American English means it was a disaster. **To table** something in British English means to bring it forward for action; in American English it means the opposite.

EXCLUSIVITY. What is familiar in one culture may be entirely alien in another. British English exploits terms and phrases borrowed from the game of cricket; American English uses baseball terms. Anyone writing for readers in both markets uses either set of terms at their peril. Do not make references or assumptions that are geographically exclusive, for example by specifying months when referring to seasonal patterns, by using north or south to imply a type of climate, or by making geographical references that give state name followed by USA, as in Wyoming, USA.

One writer's slang is another's lively use of words; formal language to one is pomposity to another. This is the trickiest area to negotiate when writing for both British and American readers. At its best, distinctively American English is more direct and vivid than its British English equivalent. Many American words and expressions have passed into British English because they are shorter or more to the point: phrases like **lay off**, preferable to **make redundant**. But American English also has a contrary tendency to lengthen words, creating a (to British readers) pompous tone: words like **transportation** (in British English, **transport**), or **obligate** (**oblige**). One American ambassador to Britain discovered this after describing his first impressions of his new home as **necessitating a degree of refurbishment**.

British English is slower than American English to accept new words, and suspicious of short cuts. In particular, it resists the use as verbs of nouns such as **author, critique, host, impact, haemorrhage, loan, party, pressure** and **roundtable**; also **gun (down)** which means **shoot**. American English, however, does not like some perfectly good words – **sufficient** is almost always **enough** and **comprise** becomes **contain, include** or **is made up of**. American English is also fast to adopt new usages for words such as **scenario, posture, parameter**.

SYNTAX AND SENTENCE STRUCTURE. American English may also use different syntax and sentence construction. Written American English tends to be more declarative than its British counterpart, and adverbs and some modifying phrases are frequently positioned differently. For example, British English may say, "**As well as going shopping, we went to the park.**" American English would turn the opening phrase around: "**We went to the park as well as going shopping**", or would begin the sentence with "**In addition to**". British English also tends to use more compound modifying phrases, while American English prefers to go with simpler sentence structure.

In British English doctors and lawyers are to be found **in** Harley Street or Wall Street, not **on** it. And they rest from their labours **at** weekends, not **on** them. During the week their children are **at** school, not **in** it.

Words may also be inserted or omitted in some standard phrases. British English goes **to hospital**, American English **to the hospital**. British English may **stop a child running into the road**, while American English would **stop it from running in the road**. British English chooses between **one or other thing**; American English chooses **one thing or the other**.

SPELLING. Some words are spelt differently; the spellings are sufficiently similar to identify the word, but the unfamiliar form may still disturb the reader. It may be better to use a synonym than to take this risk, although sometimes it cannot be avoided.

SPECIAL PROBLEMS. A number of subjects call for highly detailed, specialised guidance beyond the scope of this book, though some of the vocabulary is dealt with here. These areas include food and cookery (different names for ingredients and equipment; different systems of measurement); medicine and health care (different professional titles, drug names, therapies); human anatomy (different attitudes to the depiction of sexual organs); and gardening (different seasons and plants). Many crafts and hobbies also use different terms for equipment, materials and techniques.

–ISMS. The difficulties that arise in Europe with references to race and sex (see ETHNIC GROUPS, SEXISM) are even greater in America where readers are often more sensitive. It is currently difficult to advise how to refer to Americans whose ancestors came from Africa; preferred usage appears to be no longer **black** but there is no agreed alternative. It is totally unacceptable to refer to **American Indians** as **red**. It can also cause offence to describe the original inhabitants of the lands stretching from Greenland to Alaska as **Eskimos**; this was a corruption of a Cree word meaning **raw flesh eater**. The people themselves have at least three major tribal groupings. **Alaska native** is relatively acceptable (if in Alaska) and so is **Inuit**, though as this means men it may not last.

It is unwise to describe an adult American female as a **girl**.

A JOINT DICTIONARY

USE -IZE, NOT -ISE. The American convention is to spell with z many words that some British writers (including *The Economist*) spell with **s**. Few British readers object to this. Remember, though, that some words must end in -ise, whichever spelling convention is being followed. These include:

advertise	despise	incise
advise	devise	merchandise
apprise	disguise	premise
arise	emprise	prise
chastise	enfranchise	revise
circumcise	excise	supervise
comprise	exercise	surmise
compromise	franchise	surprise
demise	improvise	televise

Note that words with the ending -lyse, such as **analyse** and **paralyse**, should not be spelt -lyze in British English, even though they are commonly spelt thus in American English.

WORDS GENERALLY ACCEPTABLE IN BOTH BRITISH AND AMERICAN ENGLISH

ambience *not* ambiance
among *not* amongst
annex *not* annexe
artifact *not* artefact
backward *not* backwards
baptistry *not* baptistery
Bible *not* bible
Bordeaux *not* claret, for red wine of region
burned *not* burnt
bus *not* coach
busy *not* engaged, for telephones

canvases *not* canvasses
car rental *not* car hire
carryall *not* holdall
cater to *not* cater for
custom-made *not* bespoke
day nursery *not* crèche
development *not* estate, for housing
diesel fuel *not* derv
disc *not* disk, except in computing
dispatch *not* despatch

encyclopedia *not* encyclopaedia
except for *not* save
farther *not* further, for distance
first name *not* Christian name
flashlight *not* torch
flip *not* toss, for coin, etc
floor *not* storey (UK) or story (US)
focusing, focused, etc
fuel *not* petrol (UK) or gasoline (US)
forward *not* forwards
(eye)glasses *not* spectacles
grille *not* grill, for grating
gypsy *not* gipsy
hairdryer *not* hairdrier
horse-racing *not just* racing
inquire *not* enquire
insurance coverage *not* insurance cover
intermission *not* interval
jail *not* gaol
learned *not* learnt
like *not* fancy
line *not* queue
located *not* situated
location *not* situation
mathematics *not* maths (UK) or math (US)
merry-go-round *not* roundabout
motorcycle *not* motorbike
neat *not* spruce or tidy
newsstand *not* kiosk
nightgown *not* nightdress
okra *not* lady's fingers
onto *not* on to
orangeade/lemonade *not* orange/lemon squash
package *not* parcel
parking spaces/garage *not* car park (UK) or parking lot (US)
pharmacy *not* chemist (UK) or drugstore (US)
phoney *not* phony

priority *not* right of way, for vehicles
refrigerator *not* fridge
rail station *not* railway station (UK) or railroad station (US)
raincoat *not* mac, mackintosh
rent *not* hire, except for people
reservation, reserve (seats, etc) *not* booking, book
retired person *not* old-age pensioner (UK) or retiree (US)
room maid *not* chambermaid
sanatorium *not* sanitarium
slowdown *not* go-slow, in production
soccer *not* football, except for American football
sorbet *not* water-ice (UK) or sherbet (US)
spelled *not* spelt
spoiled *not* spoilt
street musician *not* busker
swap *not* swop
swimming *not* bathing
team *not* side, in sport
tearoom *not* teashop
thread *not* cotton
toilet *not* lavatory
toll-free *not* free of charge
trainers *not* plimsolls (UK) or sneakers (US)
trousers *not* pants
tuna *not* tunny
underwear *not* pants or knickers; or use lingerie for women's underwear
unmistakable *not* unmistakeable
unspoiled *not* unspoilt
while *not* whilst
whimsy, whimsies *not* whimsey, whimseys
workman *not* navvy
yogurt *not* yoghourt or yoghurt

PROBLEMATIC WORDS AND PHRASES

DIFFERENT SPELLING CONVENTIONS.
American English is more obviously phonetic than British English.
The word **cosy** becomes **cozy, aesthetic** becomes **esthetic, size-able** becomes **sizable, arbour** becomes **arbor, theatre** becomes
theater, draught becomes **draft.**
The main spelling differences between American English and
British English are as follows.

-eable/-able. The silent **e**, created when forming some adjectives
with this suffix, is more often omitted in American English; thus,
likeable is spelt **likable, unshakeable** is spelt **unshakable.** But the
e is sometimes retained in American English where it affects the
sound of the preceding consonant; thus, **traceable,** or **manageable.**

-ae/-oe. Although it is now common in British English to write
medieval rather than **mediaeval,** other words – often scientific
terms such as **aeon, diarrhoea, aesthetic, gynaecology,
homoeopathy** – retain their classical composite vowel. In American
English, the composite vowel is replaced by a single **e**; thus, **eon,
diarrhea, esthetic, gynecology, homeopathy.**

-ce/-se. In British English, the verb that relates to a noun ending in
-ce is sometimes given the ending -se; thus, **advice** (noun), **advise**
(verb), **device/devise, licence/license, practice/practise.** In the
first two instances, the spelling change is accompanied by a slight
change in the sound of the word; but in the other two instances,
noun and verb are pronounced the same way, and American English
spelling reflects this, by using the same spelling: thus, **license** and
practice. It also extends the use of -se to other nouns which in
British English are spelt -ce: thus, **defense, offense, pretense.**

-e/-ue. The final silent **e** or **ue** of several words is omitted in
American English but retained in British English: thus, **analog/ ana-
logue, ax/axe, catalog/catalogue.**

-ll/-l. In British English, when words ending in the consonant l are
given a suffix beginning with a vowel (eg, the suffixes -able, -ed,
-ing, -ous, -y), the l is doubled; thus, **annul/annulled, model/mod-
elling, quarrel/quarrelling, rebel/rebellious, wool/woolly.** This is
inconsistent with the general rule in British English that the final consonant is doubled before the suffix only when the preceding vowel
carries the main stress: thus, the word **regret** becomes **regretted,** or
regrettable; but the word **billet** becomes **billeted.** American
English mostly does not have this inconsistency. So if the stress does
not fall on the preceding vowel, the l is not doubled: thus,

model/modeling, travel/traveler; but **annul/annulled**.

Several words which end in a single l in British English – eg, **appal, fulfil** – take a double **ll** in American English. In British English, the l stays single when the word takes a suffix beginning with a consonant (eg, the suffixes -ful, -fully, -ment): thus, **fulfil/ fulfilment**. Moreover, words ending in -ll usually lose one l when taking one of these suffixes: thus, **skill/skilful, will/wilfully**. In American English, words ending in -ll usually remain intact, whatever the suffix: thus, **skill/skillful, will/willfully**.

-our/-or. Most British English words ending in -our – **ardour, behaviour, candour, demeanour, favour, valour** and the like – lose the **u** in American English: thus, **ardor, candor**, etc. The major exception is **glamour**, which retains its **u**.

-re/-er. Most British English words ending in -re – such as **centre, fibre, metre, theatre** – end in -er in American English: thus, **center, fiber**, etc. The exceptions include: **acre, cadre, lucre, massacre, mediocre, ogre**.

-t/-ed (past tense). British English uses -t – **spelt, learnt, burnt** – whereas American English uses -ed – **spelled, learned, burned**.

HYPHENATION.
American English is far readier than British English to accept compound words. In particular, many nouns made of two separate nouns are spelt as one word in American English, while in British English they would either remain separate or be joined by a hyphen: eg, **applesauce** (hyphenated in British English). British English also tends, more than American English, to use hyphens as pronunciation aids or to separate identical letters in words such as **co-operation, pre-empt, re-examine**.

American English likes hyphenated adjectives such as **in-depth, in-flight**, which although common in British English are deprecated.

COMMON PROBLEMATIC WORDS.
The following list draws attention to commonly used words and idioms that either are spelt differently or have different meanings in American English and British English. It does not cover slang or colloquialisms.

If you want to produce a single version of written material acceptable to both sorts of readers, you should avoid using the words in this list when there is a mutually acceptable alternative (see pages 76–77). If not, follow one or other convention, and, if this means using a word that will mystify or mislead one group of readers, provide a translation.

British	American
accommodation (lodging/s)	accommodation/s (lodging/s)
adopt (a candidate)	nominate
aerial (TV)	antenna
air hostess	flight attendant
aluminium	aluminum
anti-clockwise	counterclockwise
apophthegm	apothegm
apple purée	applesauce
at weekends	on weekends
aubergine	eggplant
autumn	fall
baby's dummy	pacifier
baking tray	baking sheet
bag, handbag	purse, pocketbook
banknote	bill
barrister	trial lawyer
behind	in back of
behove	behoove
bicarbonate of soda	baking soda
bilberry	blueberry
bill	check
biscuit (sweet)	cookie
biscuit (savoury)	cracker
black treacle	molasses
blind (for windows)	shade
bowler (hat)	derby
braces	suspenders
building society	savings and loan association
calibre	caliber
camp bed	cot
car, estate	station wagon
car, saloon	sedan
car accelerator	gas pedal
car bonnet	hood
car boot	trunk
car demister	defogger
car dipswitch	dimmer
car jump leads	jumper cables
car park	parking lot
car silencer	muffler
car windscreen	windshield
car wing	fender
caravan	house trailer
cheque (bank)	check
chequered	checkered (pattern)

British	American
chickpea	garbanzo bean
chilli/chillies	chili/chilis
chips	French fries
choux bun	cream puff
cinema	movie theater
clever	smart
cling film	plastic wrap
coach	bus
coriander (fresh)	cilantro
corn	wheat
cornflour	cornstarch
cosy	cozy
cot	crib
country	nation
courgette	zucchini
crayfish	crawfish
crisps	chips
crossroads/junction	intersection
crystallized	candied
cupboard/wardrobe	closet
demerara sugar	light-brown sugar
desiccated coconut	shredded coconut
dialled	dialed
diary (appointments)	calendar
diary (record)	journal
digestive biscuit	graham cracker
district	neighborhood
doctor	physician
double cream	heavy cream
draught	draft
dressing gown	bathrobe/housecoat
drug	narcotic
dual carriageway	four-lane (or divided) highway
dyke	dike
essence (eg, vanilla)	extract or flavoring
estate agent	realtor/real estate agent
ex-serviceman	veteran
eyrie	aerie
flan tin	pie pan
flat	apartment
fillet (boneless meat/fish)	filet
flour, plain	flour, all-purpose
flour, self-raising	flour, self-rising
flour, wholemeal	flour, whole-wheat
flyover	overpass
from ... to ...	through

British	American
frying pan	skillet
fuelled	fueled
full stop (punctuation)	period
furore	furor
give way	yield
golden syrup	corn syrup
greengrocer's	vegetable market
grey	gray
grill (verb and noun)	broil (verb), broiler (noun)
ground floor	first floor
high street	main street
hire (of car)	rent
holiday	vacation (*but* public holiday)
home from home	home away from home
homely	homey/homy (homely = plain)
icing sugar	powdered or confectioners' sugar
in (Fifth Avenue, etc)	on
increase	hike
jeweller/jewellery	jeweler/jewelry
jumper	sweater
keep a promise	deliver (on a promise)
kerb/kerbside	curb/curbside
ketchup	catsup
labelled	labeled
ladder (in stocking)	run
lawyer	attorney
lease of life	lease on life
lent	loaned
lift	elevator
liquidiser	blender
lorry	truck
lustre	luster
maize/sweetcorn	corn
manoeuvre/manoeuvrable	maneuver/maneuverable
mean (parsimonious)	stingy, tight (mean = nasty)
meet	meet with
metre (unit of distance)	meter
minced meat	ground meat
modelled	modeled
motor-racing	auto-racing
motorway	superhighway, freeway, expressway
mould/moulder/moult	mold/molder/molt
moustache	mustache
mum/mummy	mom/mommy
muslin	cheesecloth

British	American
nappy	diaper
nervy	nervous (nervy = brazen)
nominate, predict	slate
oblige	obligate
omelette	omelet
ordinary	regular, normal
outside	outside of
paddling pool	wading pool
panelled	wood-paneled
pants	underpants
pastry case	pie shell
pavement	sidewalk
pepper (red, green, etc)	capsicum or sweet pepper
petrol	gasoline, gas
petrol station	gas/service station
pips	seeds (in fruit)
pitta bread	pita bread
plain/dark chocolate	semisweet or unsweetened chocolate
plait	braid
plough	plow
podgy	pudgy
polythene	polyethylene
post, post box	mail, mailbox
power point	electrical outlet
pram, push chair	stroller
programme (except computer)	program
property (land)	real estate
pumpkin	squash
pyjamas	pajamas
queue	line, line up
quitted (past tense and participle of quit)	quit
rambler	hiker
removal van	moving van
request stop	flag stop
rationalisation	downsizing
riding (horses)	horseback riding
ring road	beltway
rivalled	rivaled
rowing boat	rowboat
run in (car, engine)	break in
scallywag	scalawag
sceptical	skeptical
senior	ranking (sometimes)
shortcrust pastry	pie dough

83

British	American
shorthand typist	stenographer
single cream	light cream
sizeable	sizable
skilful	skillful
sleepers	railroad ties
smoulder	smolder
soda water	seltzer
solicitor	attorney
sombre	somber
soya	soy
spanner	wrench
specialist shop	specialty shop
speciality (*but* specialty for medicine, steel and chemicals)	specialty
sponge finger biscuits	ladyfingers
spring onion	scallion
stand (for election)	run
stocks	inventory
stone	rock
stoned (cherries, etc)	pitted
storey (of building)	story
stupid	dumb
subway	pedestrian underpass
sulphur(ous)	sulfur(ous)
sultana	golden (seedless) raisin
suspenders	garters
sweated (past tense and participle of sweat)	sweat
sweet shop	candy store
tap	faucet
terraced house	row house
till	check-out
titbit	tidbit
tomato purée	tomato paste
towards	toward
transport	transportation
traveller/travelled	traveler/traveled
trousers	pants or slacks
trunk call	long-distance call
turning (road)	turnoff
tyre	tire
underground (or tube train)	subway
upmarket	upscale
vest	undershirt
vice (tool)	vise

British	American
waistcoat	vest
walk	hike
water biscuit	cracker
way out	exit
woollen/woolly	woolen/wooly
work out (problem)	figure out
zip	zipper

DIFFERENCES IN PUNCTUATION

COMMA IN LISTS. Americans often put a comma before the **and**: **eggs, bacon, potatoes, and cheese.** The British more often write **eggs, bacon, potatoes and cheese.**

DASHES. In British publications, the usual style for a dash used as a parenthesis is an en-rule (–) with a character space either side. In American publications, the usual style for a dash is an em-rule (—) with no spaces.

FULL STOPS (PERIOD). The American convention is to use full stops (periods) to identify almost all abbreviations. The British convention is to keep them to a minimum.

QUOTATION MARKS. In American publications (and those of major Commonwealth countries), the convention is to use double quotation marks, reserving single quotation marks for quotes within quotes. In British publications, the convention is the reverse (except in *The Economist*): single quotation marks are used first, then double. However, the American style is becoming more popular.

The relative position of quotation marks and other punctuation is far more contentious. The British convention is to place such punctuation according to sense. The American convention is simpler but less logical: all commas and full stops precede the final quotation mark (or, if there is a quote within a quote, the first final quotation mark). Other punctuation – colons, semi-colons, question and exclamation marks – is placed according to sense. The following examples illustrate the differences.

American style
The words on the magazine's cover, "The link between coffee and cholesterol," caught his eye.
"You're eating too much," she told him. "You'll soon look like your father."
"Have you seen this article, 'The link between coffee and cholesterol'?" he asked.

"It was as if," he explained, "I had swallowed a toad, and it kept croaking 'ribbut, ribbut,' from deep in my stomach."

She particularly enjoyed the article "Looking for the 'New Man.' "

British style

The words on the magazine's cover, 'The link between coffee and cholesterol', caught his eye.

'You're eating too much,' she told him. 'You'll soon look like your father.'

'Have you seen this article, "The link between coffee and cholesterol"?' he asked.

'It was as if,' he explained, 'I had swallowed a toad, and it kept croaking "ribbut, ribbut", from deep in my belly.'

She particularly enjoyed the article 'Looking for the "New Man" '.

DIFFERENT UNITS OF MEASUREMENT

In British publications measurements are now largely expressed in SI units (the modern form of metric units), although imperial measures are still used in certain contexts. In American publications measurements may be expressed in SI or imperial units.

Although in most cases the British imperial and American standard measures are identical, there are some important exceptions. There are also some measures peculiar to one or other national system, particularly units of mass relating to agriculture. See also MEASUREMENTS (Part I) and MEASURES (Part III).

PART III

FACT CHECKER
AND
GLOSSARY

A

ABBREVIATIONS.
Here is a list of some common business abbreviations. (See also
ABBREVIATIONS, pages 10–11.)

ACA	Associate of the Institute of Chartered Accountants in England and Wales, or Ireland
ACT	advance corporation tax (UK)
AG	Aktiengesellschaft (German or Swiss public limited company)
AGM	annual general meeting
AIM	Alternative Investment Market (UK)
APR	annual percentage rate
ASSC	Accounting Standards Steering Committee (UK)
CA	member of the Institute of Chartered Accountants of Scotland
CAPM	capital asset pricing model
CCA	current cost accounting
CGT	capital gains tax
cif	cost, insurance, freight
COB	Commission des Opérations de Bourse (Stock Exchange Commission, France)
Consob	Commissione Nazionale per le Società e la Borsa (Stock Exchange Commission, Italy)
CPA	certified public accountant (USA); critical path analysis
CPP	current purchasing power (accounting)
CTT	capital transfer tax
DCF	discounted cash flow
ECU	European currency unit
EFT	electronic funds transfer
EFTPOS	electronic funds transfer at point of sale
EMS	European Monetary System
EMU	economic and monetary union
EPS	earnings per share
ERM	exchange-rate mechanism
EU	European Union
FASB	Financial Accounting Standards Board (USA)
FCA	Fellow of the Institute of Chartered Accountants in England and Wales, or Ireland
fob	free on board
GAAP	generally accepted accounting principles (USA)
GmbH	Gesellschaft mit beschränkter Haftung (German or Swiss

private limited company)

IRR	internal rate of return
IRS	Internal Revenue Service (USA)
LIFFE	London International Financial Futures Exchange
MCT	mainstream corporation tax
MLR	minimum lending rate
NASDAQ	National Association of Securities Dealers Automated Quotations System (USA)
NPV	net present value; no par value
NYSE	New York Stock Exchange
Nymex	New York Mercantile Exchange
NRV	net realisable value
P/E	price/earnings ratio
P&L a/c	profit and loss account
PLC	public limited company (UK)
PRT	petroleum revenue tax (UK)
PSBR	public-sector borrowing rate
R&D	research and development
ROCE	return on capital employed
ROI	return on investment
SA	société anonyme (French, Belgian, Luxembourg or Swiss public limited company)
Sarl	société à responsabilité limitée (French, etc private limited company)
SEAQ	Stock Exchange Automated Quotation System (UK)
SEC	Securities and Exchange Commission (USA)
SERPS	state earnings-related pension scheme
SIB	Securities and Investments Board (UK)
SRO	self-regulating organisation
SSAP	Statement of Standard Accounting Practice (UK)
UEC	Union Européenne des Experts Comptables Economiques et Financiers
VAT	value-added tax
ZBB	zero base budgeting

For international bodies and their abbreviations, see ORGANISATIONS (pages 124ff).

ACCENTS. Here are some of the more familiar foreign language accents.

acute	république
grave	grand'mère
circumflex	bête noire
umlaut	Länder, Österreich (Austria)
cedilla	français
tilde	señor, São Paulo

ACCOUNTANCY RATIOS.

These are the ratios most commonly used in accounting practice.

Working capital

Working capital ratio = current assets/current liabilities, where current assets = stock + debtors + cash at bank and in hand + quoted investments, etc, current liabilities = creditors + overdraft at bank + taxation + dividends, etc. The ratio varies according to type of trade and conditions; a ratio from 1 to 3 is usual with a ratio above 2 being generally good.

Liquidity ratio = liquid ("quick") assets/current liabilities, where liquid assets = debtors + cash at bank and in hand + quoted investments (that is assets which can be realised within a month or so, which may not apply to all investments); current liabilities are those which may need to be repaid within the same short period, which may not necessarily include a bank overdraft where it is likely to be renewed. The liquidity ratio is sometimes referred to as the "acid test"; a ratio under 1 suggests a possibly difficult situation, while too high a ratio may mean that assets are not being usefully employed.

Turnover of working capital = sales/average working capital. The ratio varies according to type of trade; generally a low ratio can mean poor use of resources, while too high a ratio can mean over-trading.

Turnover of stock = sales/average stock, or (where cost of sales is known) = cost of sales/average stock. The cost of sales turnover figure is to be preferred as both figures are then on the same valuation basis. This ratio can be expressed as number of times per year, or time taken for stock to be turned over once = (52/number of times) weeks. A low turnover of stock can be a sign of stocks which are difficult to move, and is usually a sign of adverse conditions.

Turnover of debtors = credit sales/average debtors. This indicates efficiency in collecting accounts. An average "credit period" of about one month is usual, but varies according to credit stringency conditions in the economy.

Turnover of creditors = purchases/average creditors. Average payment period is best maintained in line with turnover of debtors.

Sales

Export ratio = exports as a percentage of sales.
Sales per employee = sales/average number of employees.

Assets

Ratios of assets can vary according to the measure of assets used:
Total assets = current assets + fixed assets + other assets, where fixed assets = property + plant and machinery + motor vehicles, etc, and other assets = long-term investment + goodwill, etc.
Net assets ("net worth") = total assets - total liabilities
                            = share capital + reserves

Turnover of net assets = sales/average net assets. As for turnover of working capital, a low ratio can mean poor use of resources.

Assets per employee = assets/average number of employees. Indicates the amount of investment backing for employees.

Profits

Profit margin = (profit/sales) x 100 = profits as a percentage of sales; usually profits before tax.

Profitability = (profit/total assets) x 100 = profits as a percentage of total assets.

Return on capital = (profit/net assets) x 100 = profits as a percentage of net assets ("net worth" or "capital employed").

B

BEAUFORT SCALE. The Beaufort Scale, once a picturesque fleet of well-scrubbed men-o'-war and fishing smacks, has been rendered bland by the World Meteorological Organization.

BEAUFORT SCALE

The Beaufort Scale

Conditions (abbreviated)

Force	Description	On land	At sea	Equivalent speed at 10m height		
				knots	miles per hour	metres per second
0	Calm	Smoke rises vertically	Sea like a mirror	less than 1	less than 1	0.0–0.2
1	Light air	Smoke drifts	Ripples	1–3	1–3	0.3–1.5
2	Light breeze	Leaves rustle	Small wavelets	4–6	4–7	1.7–3.3
3	Gentle breeze	Wind extends light flag	Large wavelets, crests break	7–10	8–12	3.4–5.4
4	Moderate breeze	Raises paper and dust	Small waves, some white horses	11–16	13–18	5.5–7.9
5	Fresh breeze	Small trees in leaf sway	Moderate waves, many white horses	17–21	19–24	8.0–10.7
6	Strong breeze	Large branches in motion	Large waves form, some spray	22–27	25–31	10.8–13.8
7	Moderate gale or near gale	Whole trees in motion	Sea heaps up, white foam streaks	28–33	32–38	13.9–17.1
8	Fresh gale or gale	Breaks twigs off trees	Moderately high waves, well-marked foam streaks	34–40	39–46	17.2–20.7
9	Strong gale	Slight structural damage to tumble over	High waves, crests start	41–47	47–54	20.8–24.4
10	Whole gale or storm	Trees uprooted, considerable structural damage	Very high waves, white sea tumbles	48–55	55–63	24.5–28.4
11	Storm or violent storm	Very rarely experienced, widespread damage	Exceptionally high waves, edges of wave crests blown to froth	56–63	64–72	28.5–32.6
12–17	Hurricane	Devastation with driving spray	Sea completely white	64–118	73–136	32.7–over

93

C

CALENDARS.
There are six important solar calendars.

Gregorian	Iranian[b]	Hindu[c]
January (31)[a]		
February (28 or 29)		
March (31)	Favardin (31)	Caitra (30)
April (30)	Ordibehesht (31)	Vaisakha (31)
May (31)	Khordad (31)	Jyaistha (31)
June (30)	Tir (31)	Asadha (31)
July (31)	Mordad (31)	Sravana (31)
August (31)	Sharivar (31)	Bhadrapada (31)
September (30)	Mehr (30)	Asvina (30)
October (31)	Aban (30)	Karttika (30)
November (30)	Azar (30)	Margasirsa (30)
December (31)	Dey (30)	Pausa (30)
(January)	Bahman (30)	Magha (30)
(February)	Esfand (28 or 29)	Phalguna (30)

Gregorian	Ethiopian[d]	Jewish[e]
September (30)	Maskerem (30)	Tishri (30)
October (31)	Tikimit (30)	Cheshvan (29 or 30)
November (30)	Hidar (30)	Kislev (29 or 30)
December (31)	Tahsas (30)	Tebet (29)
(January)	Tir (30)	Shebat (30)
(February)	Yekatit (30)	Adar (29)
(March)	Megabit (30)	Nisan (30)
(April)	Miazia (30)	Iyyar (29)
(May)	Guenbot (30)	Sivan (30)
(June)	Sene (30)	Tammuz (29)
(July)	Hamle (30)	Ab (30)
(August)	Nahassie (30+5 or 6)	Elul (29)

[a] Figures in brackets denote the number of days in that month.
[b] Months begin about the 21st of the corresponding Gregorian month.
[c] Months begin about the 22nd of the corresponding Gregorian month.
[d] Months begin on the 11th of the corresponding Gregorian month.
[e] The date of the new year varies, but normally falls in the second half of September in the Gregorian calendar; the general calendar position is maintained by adding, in some years, an extra period of 29 days, Adar Sheni, following the month of Adar.

The Muslim calendar. Muslims use a lunar calendar which begins 10 or 11 days earlier each year in terms of the Gregorian. The months do not, however, have a fixed number of days. The priesthood declares the official start of each month. The names of the months are as follows.

Muharram	Rajab
Safar	Shaaban
Rabia I	Ramadan
Rabia II	Shawwal
Jumada I	Dhu al-Kadah
Jumada II	Dhu al-Hijjah

In each 30 years, 19 years have 354 days (are "common") and 11 have 355 days (are "intercalary").

Muslim years begin on the following dates of the Gregorian calendar.

1411	July 24th 1990
1412	July 13th 1991
1413	July 2nd 1992
1414	June 21st 1993
1415	June 9th 1994
1416	May 31st 1995
1417	May 19th 1996
1418	May 9th 1997

CARS.

Here is a list of some international vehicle registration (IVR) letters.

A	Austria	FIN	Finland
AUS	Australia	GB	Great Britain
B	Belgium	GR	Greece
BD	Bangladesh	H	Hungary
BR	Brazil	HK	Hong Kong
CAM	Cameroon	I	Italy
CDN	Canada	IL	Israel
CH	Switzerland	IND	India
CI	Côte d'Ivoire	IR	Iran
CO	Colombia	IRL	Ireland
CZ	Czech Republic	IRQ	Iraq
D	Germany	J	Japan
DK	Denmark	MA	Morocco
DZ	Algeria	MAL	Malaysia
E	Spain	MEX	Mexico
EAK	Kenya	N	Norway
ET	Egypt	NL	Netherlands
F	France	NZ	New Zealand

P	Portugal	SA	Saudi Arabia
PK	Pakistan	SK	Slovakia
PE	Peru	SGP	Singapore
PI	Philippines	SLO	Slovenia
PL	Poland	T	Thailand
RA	Argentina	TR	Turkey
RC	Taiwan	USA	United States of
RCH	Chile		America
RI	Indonesia	WAN	Nigeria
RO	Romania	YV	Venezuela
ROK	South Korea	ZA	South Africa
RUS	Russia	ZRE	Zaire
S	Sweden	ZW	Zimbabwe

CITIES. Correct spellings of some of the cities of the world with populations of more than 2m are listed here. These may be conurbations rather than metropolitan areas. Cities marked [a] are capital cities.

Ahmadabad	*India*	Harbin	*China*
Aleppo	*Syria*	Havana[a]	*Cuba*
Alexandria	*Egypt*	Ho Chi Minh City	
Ankara[a]	*Turkey*	(Saigon)	*Vietnam*
Athens[a]	*Greece*	Hong Kong[a]	*Hong Kong*
Baghdad[a]	*Iraq*	Houston	*USA*
Bangalore	*India*	Hyderabad	*India*
Bangkok	*Thailand*	Ibadan	*Nigeria*
Beijing[a] (Peking)	*China*	Istanbul	*Turkey*
Bogota[a]	*Colombia*	Jakarta[a]	*Indonesia*
Bombay	*India*	Karachi	*Pakistan*
Boston	*USA*	Kiev[a]	*Ukraine*
Budapest[a]	*Hungary*	Kinshasa[a]	*Zaire*
Buenos Aires[a]	*Argentina*	Lagos	*Nigeria*
Cairo[a]	*Egypt*	Lahore	*Pakistan*
Calcutta	*India*	Lima[a]	*Peru*
Caracas[a]	*Venezuela*	London[a]	*UK*
Casablanca	*Morocco*	Los Angeles	*USA*
Chengdu	*China*	Madras	*India*
Chicago	*USA*	Madrid[a]	*Spain*
Chongqing	*China*	Manila[a]	*Philippines*
Dacca	*Bangladesh*	Melbourne	*Australia*
Dallas	*USA*	Mexico City[a]	*Mexico*
Damascus[a]	*Syria*	Monterrey	*Mexico*
Delhi[a]	*India*	Montreal	*Canada*
Detroit	*USA*	Moscow[a]	*Russia*
Guadalajara	*Mexico*	Nagoya	*Japan*
Guangzhou (Canton)	*China*	Nanjing	*China*
Hanoi[a]	*Vietnam*	New York	*USA*

Osaka	*Japan*	Singapore[a]	*Singapore*
Paris[a]	*France*	Surabaya	*Indonesia*
Philadelphia	*USA*	Sydney	*Australia*
Pusan	*South Korea*	Taegu	*South Korea*
Pyongyang	*North Korea*	Taipei[a]	*Taiwan*
Rio de Janeiro	*Brazil*	Tashkent[a]	*Uzbekistan*
Rome[a]	*Italy*	Tehran[a]	*Iran*
St Petersburg	*Russia*	Tianjin	*China*
San Francisco	*USA*	Tokyo[a]	*Japan*
Santiago[a]	*Chile*	Toronto	*Canada*
Santo Domingo[a]		Shanghai	*China*
	Dominican Republic	Washington[a]	*USA*
Sao Paulo	*Brazil*	Wuhan	*China*
Shanghai	*China*	Xi'an	*China*
Shenyang	*China*	Yangon[a]	*Myanmar*
Seoul[a]	*South Korea*	Yokohama	*Japan*

COMMODITIES AND MANUFACTURED GOODS.
Most countries use the Standard International Trade Classification (SITC) to describe the goods they import and trade. The classifications are periodically revised: SITC (3) was introduced in January 1988. A list of the main items follows.

There are 9 sections, giving single digits 1–9; divisions within these sections have 2-digit numbers, and groups within each division have 3-digit numbers. In the list below all sections and divisions are shown together with selected groups. There are also 4-digit subgroups in the SITC list, with, for example, 072.3 for "cocoa paste" as a subgroup of 072 ("cocoa"), and further breakdowns for some items into a 5-digit level, with, for example, 072.32 for "cocoa paste, wholly or partly defatted".

Throughout, nes stands for "not elsewhere specified".

0	Food and live animals
00	Live animals other than animals of division 03
01	Meat and meat preparations
02	Dairy products and birds' eggs
022	Milk and cream and milk products other than butter or cheese
023	Butter and other fats and oils derived from milk
024	Cheese and curd
03	Fish (not marine mammals), crustaceans, molluscs and aquatic invertebrates, and preparations thereof
04	Cereal and cereal production
041	Wheat (including spelt) and meslin, unmilled
042	Rice
043	Barley, unmilled
044	Maize (not including sweetcorn), unmilled

05	Vegetables and fruit
06	Sugar, sugar preparations and honey
07	Coffee, tea, cocoa, spices, and manufactures thereof
071	Coffee and coffee substitutes
072	Cocoa
074	Tea and maté
08	Feeding stuff for animals (not including unmilled cereals)
09	Miscellaneous edible products and preparations

1	Beverages and tobacco
11	Beverages
112	Alcoholic beverages
12	Tobacco and tobacco manufactures

2	Crude materials, inedible, except fuels
21	Hides, skins and furskins, raw
22	Oil seeds and oleaginous fruit
23	Crude rubber (including synthetic and reclaimed)
24	Cork and wood
25	Pulp and waste paper
26	Textile fibres (other than wool tops), and their wastes (not manufactured into yarn or fabric)
263	Cotton
266	Synthetic fibres suitable for spinning
267	Other man-made fibres suitable for spinning and waste of man-made fibres
268	Wool and other animal hair (including wool tops)
27	Crude fertilisers other than those of division 56 and crude minerals (excluding coal, petroleum and precious stones)
28	Metalliferous ores and metal scrap
281	Iron ore and concentrates
29	Crude animal and vegetable materials, nes

3	Mineral fuels, lubricants and related materials
32	Coal, coke and briquettes
33	Petroleum, petroleum products, and related materials
333	Petroleum oils and oils obtained from bituminous materials, crude
34	Gas, natural and manufactured
35	Electric current

4	Animal and vegetable oils, fats and waxes
41	Animal oils and fats
42	Fixed vegetable fats and oils; crude, refined or fractioned
43	Animal and vegetable oils and fats, processed and waxes of animal or vegetable origin; inedible mixtures or preparations of animal or vegetable fats and oils, nes

5	Chemical and related products, nes
51	Organic chemicals
52	Inorganic chemicals
53	Dyeing, tanning and colouring materials
54	Medicinal and pharmaceutical products
55	Essential oils, resinoids and perfume materials; toilet, polishing and cleansing preparations
56	Fertilisers (other than those of group 27)
57	Plastics in primary forms
58	Plastics in non-primary forms
59	Chemical materials and products, nes
6	Manufactured goods, classified chiefly by material
61	Leather, leather manufactures, nes and dressed furskins
62	Rubber manufactures, nes
63	Cork and wood manufactures (excluding furniture)
64	Paper, paperboard and articles of paper pulp, of paper or of paperboard
65	Textile yarn, fabrics, made-up articles, nes and related products
66	Non-metallic mineral manufactures, nes
67	Iron and steel
68	Non-ferrous metals
681	Silver, platinum and other metals of the platinum group
682	Copper
683	Nickel
684	Aluminium
687	Tin
69	Manufactures of metal, nes
7	Machinery and transport equipment
71	Power generating machinery and equipment
713	Internal combustion piston engines, and parts thereof, nes
72	Machinery specialised for particular industries
721	Agricultural machinery (excluding tractors) and parts thereof
724	Textile and leather machinery, and parts thereof, nes
73	Metalworking machinery
74	General industrial machinery and equipment, nes, and machine parts, nes
75	Office machines and automatic data processing machines
76	Telecommunications, sound recording and reproducing apparatus and equipment
761	Television receivers (including monitors and projectors) whether or not incorporating radio receivers or recording/reproducing apparatus
77	Electrical machinery, apparatus and appliances, nes and electrical parts thereof (including non-electrical counterparts,

nes, of electrical household-type equipment)

78   Road vehicles (including air cushion vehicles)
781   Motor cars and other motor vehicles principally designed for
      the transport of persons (other than public transport vehicles
782   Motor vehicles for the transport of goods and special
      purpose motor vehicles
79   Other transport equipment
791   Railway vehicles (including hovertrains) and associated
      equipment
792   Aircraft and associated equipment; spacecraft (including
      satellites) and spacecraft launch vehicles
793   Ships, boats (including hovercraft) and floating structures

8   Miscellaneous manufactured articles
81   Prefabricated buildings; sanitary, plumbing, heating and
      lighting fixtures and fittings, nes
82   Furniture and parts thereof; bedding, mattresses, supports,
      cushions and similar stuffed furnishings
83   Travel goods, handbags and similar containers
84   Articles of apparel and clothing accessories
85   Footwear
87   Professional, scientific and controlling instruments and
      apparatus, nes
88   Photographic apparatus, equipment and supplies and optical
      goods, nes; watches and clocks
881   Photographic apparatus and equipment, nes
885   Watches and clocks
89   Miscellaneous manufactured articles, nes

9   Commodities and transactions not classified elsewhere in the
      SITC
911   Postal packages not classified according to kind
931   Special transactions and commodities not classified
      according to kind
961   Coin (other than gold coin) not being legal tender
981   Military arms and ammunitions

CURRENCIES.

Country	Currency	Symbol[a]
Afghanistan	afghani	Af
Albania	lek	Lk
Algeria	Algerian dinar	AD
Angola	kwanza	Kz
Argentina	peso	PS
Armenia	dram	–
Australia	Australian dollar	A$
Austria	schilling	Sch
Azerbaijan	manat	–
Bahamas	Bahamian dollar	B$
Bahrain	Bahrain dinar	BD
Bangladesh	taka	Tk
Barbados	Barbadian dollar	Bd$
Belgium	Belgian franc	BFr
Belarus	rouble	Rbl
Belize	Belizean dollar	Bz$
Benin	CFA franc	CFAfr
Bermuda	Bermuda dollar	Bda$
Bhutan	ngultrum	Nu
Bolivia	Boliviano	Bol
Botswana	pula	P
Brazil	cruzeiro	Cr
Brunei	Brunei dollar	Br$
Bulgaria	lev	Lv
Burkina Faso	CFA franc	CFAfr
Burundi	Burundi franc	Bufr
Cambodia	riel	CR
Cameroon	CFA franc	CFAfr
Canada	Canadian dollar	C$
Cape Verde	Cape Verde escudo	CVEsc
Central African Republic	CFA franc	CFAfr
Chad	CFA franc	CFAfr
Chile	Chilean peso	peso
China	yuan	Y
Colombia	Colombian peso	peso
Comoros	Comoran franc	Cfr
Congo	CFA franc	CFAfr
Costa Rica	Costa Rican colón	¢
Côte d'Ivoire	CFA franc	CFAfr
Croatia	kuna	HRK
Cuba	Cuban peso	peso
Cyprus	Cyprus pound	C£
Czech Republic	koruna	Kcs

Country	Currency	Symbol[a]
Denmark	Danish krone	DKr
Djibouti	Djibouti franc	Dfr
Dominican Republic	Dominican Republic peso	peso
Ecuador	sucre	Su
Egypt	Egyptian pound	£E
El Salvador	El Salvador colón	¢
Equatorial Guinea	CFA franc	CFAfr
Estonia	kroon	EEK
Ethiopia	birr	Birr
Fiji	Fiji dollar	F$
Finland	markka	Fmk
France	franc	Fr
Gabon	CFA franc	CFAfr
The Gambia	dalasi	D
Georgia	lari	–
Germany	Deutschemark	DM
Ghana	cedi	C
Greece	drachma	Dr
Guatemala	quetzal	Q
Guinea	Guinean franc	Gfr
Guinea Bissau	Guinea Bissau peso	P
Guyana	Guyanese dollar	G$
Haiti	gourde	gourdes
Honduras	lempira	La
Hong Kong	Hong Kong dollar	HK$
Hungary	forint	Ft
Iceland	Icelandic krona	Ikr
India	Indian rupee	Rs
Indonesia	rupiah	Rp
Iran	rial	IR
Iraq	Iraqi dinar	ID
Ireland	Irish pound (punt)	I£
Israel	new shekel	NIS
Italy	lira (pl. lire)	L
Jamaica	Jamaican dollar	J$
Japan	yen	¥
Jordan	Jordan dinar	JD
Kazakhstan	tenge	–
Kenya	Kenya shilling	KSh
Kirgizstan	som	–
North Korea	won	Won
South Korea	won	W
Kuwait	Kuwaiti dinar	KD
Laos	kip	K
Latvia	lat	–

Country	Currency	Symbol[a]
Lebanon	Lebanese pound	L£
Lesotho	loti (pl. maloti)	M
Liberia	Liberian dollar	L$
Libya	Libyan dinar	LD
Lithuania	lit	–
Luxembourg	Luxembourg franc	Lfr
Macau	pataca	MPtc
Madagascar	Madagascar franc	Mgfr
Malawi	kwacha	MK
Malaysia	Malaysian dollar/ringgit	M$
Mali	CFA franc	CFAfr
Malta	Maltese lira	Lm
Mauritania	ouguiya	UM
Mauritius	Mauritius rupee	MRs
Mexico	Mexican peso	peso
Moldova	Rouble	Rbl
Morocco	dirham	Dh
Mozambique	metical	MT
Myanmar	kyat	Kt
Namibia	South African rand	R
Nepal	Nepalese rupee	NRs
Netherlands	guilder	G
Netherlands Antilles	Netherlands Antilles guilder	NAG
New Zealand	New Zealand dollar	NZ$
Nicaragua	córdoba	C
Niger	CFA franc	CFAfr
Nigeria	naira	N
Norway	Norwegian krone	NKr
Oman	Omani rial	OR
Pakistan	Pakistan rupee	PRs
Panama	balboa	B
Papua New Guinea	Kina	Kina
Paraguay	guarani	G
Peru	inti	In
Philippines	Philippine peso	P
Poland	zloty	Zl
Portugal	escudo	Esc
Puerto Rico	US dollar	$
Qatar	Qatari riyal	QR
Romania	leu (pl. lei)	Lei
Russia	Rouble	Rbl
Rwanda	Rwandan franc	Rwfr
São Tomé & Príncipe	dobra	Db
Saudi Arabia	Saudi riyal	SR
Senegal	CFA franc	CFAfr

Country	Currency	Symbol[a]
Seychelles	Seychelles rupee	SRs
Sierra Leone	leone	Le
Singapore	Singaporean dollar	S$
Slovakia	koruna	Kcs
Slovenia	tolar	–
Solomon Islands	Solomon Island dollar	SI$
Somalia	Somali shilling	SoSh
South Africa	rand	R
Spain	peseta	Pta
Sri Lanka	Sri Lanka rupee	SLRs
Sudan	Sudanese pound	S£
Suriname	Suriname guilder	SG
Swaziland	lilangeni (pl. emalengeni)	E
Sweden	Swedish krona	SKr
Switzerland	Swiss franc	SFr
Syria	Syrian pound	S£
Taiwan	New Taiwanese dollar	NT$
Tanzania	Tanzanian shilling	TSh
Thailand	baht	Bt
Togo	CFA franc	CFAfr
Tonga	Tonga dollar	T$
Trinidad & Tobago	Trinidad & Tobago dollar	TT$
Tunisia	Tunisian dinar	TD
Turkey	Turkish lira	TL
Turkmenistan	manat	–
Uganda	New Ugandan shilling	NUSh
Ukraine	karbovanets	Kb
United Arab Emirates	UAE dirham	Dh
United Kingdom	pound/sterling	£
United States of America	dollar	$
Uruguay	Uruguayan new peso	peso
Vanuatu	vatu	Vt
Venezuela	bolívar	Bs
Vietnam	dong	D
Western Samoa	Tala	Tala
Windward & Leewards[b]	East Caribbean dollar	EC$
Yemen	Yemeni rial	YR
Yugoslavia (former)	New dinar	YuD
Zaire	zaire	Z
Zambia	Zambian kwacha	ZK
Zimbabwe	Zimbabwe dollar	Z$

a See CURRENCIES for *The Economist* newspaper usage.

b Antigua & Barbuda, Dominica, Grenada, Monserrat, St Kitts-Nevis, St Lucia, St Vincent & Grenadines, the British Virgin islands.

E

EARTHQUAKES. The Richter scale defines the magnitude of an earthquake in terms of the energy released.

Richter scale			Explosion equivalent	
	Joules		TNT terms	Nuclear terms
0[a]	7.9	x 10^2	175mg	
1	6.0	x 10^4	13g	
2	4.0	x 10^6	0.89kg	
3	2.4	x 10^8	53kg	
4	1.3	x 10^{10}	3 tons	
5[b]	6.3	x 10^{11}	140 tons	
6[c]	2.7	x 10^{13}	6 kilotons	$^1/_3$ atomic bomb
7	1.1	x 10^{15}	240 kilotons	12 atomic bombs
8	3.7	x 10^{16}	8.25 megatons	$^1/_3$ hydrogen bomb
9	1.1	x 10^{18}	250 megatons	13 hydrogen bombs
10	3.2	x 10^{19}	7,000 megatons	350 hydrogen bombs

a Approximately equal to the shock caused by an average man jumping from a table.
b Potentially damaging to structures.
c Potentially capable of general destruction; widespread damage is usually caused above magnitude 6.5.

Note: One atomic bomb is equivalent to 6.3 on the Richter scale, and one hydrogen bomb to 8.2.

Here are some examples.

	Richter scale
Northridge, CA, 1994	6.7
Kobe, Japan, 1995	6.9
Mexico City, 1986	7.8
San Francisco, 1906	8.3
Chile, 1960	8.3
Krakatoa, 1883	9.9 (estimate)

ELEMENTS.
These are the natural and artificially created chemical elements.

Name	Symbol	Name	Symbol
Actinium	Ac	Iridium	Ir
Aluminium	Al	Iron (Ferrum)	Fe
Americium	Am	Krypton	Kr
Antimony (Stibium)	Sb	Lanthanum	La
Argon	Ar	Lawrencium	Lr
Arsenic	As	Lead (Plumbum)	Pb
Astatine	At	Lithium	Li
Barium	Ba	Lutetium	Lu
Berkelium	Bk	Magnesium	Mg
Beryllium	Be	Manganese	Mn
Bismuth	Bi	Mendelevium	Md
Boron	B	Mercury (Hydrargyrum)	Hg
Bromine	Br	Molybdenum	Mo
Cadmium	Cd	Neodymium	Nd
Caesium	Cs	Neon	Ne
Calcium	Ca	Neptunium	Np
Californium	Cf	Nickel	Ni
Carbon	C	Niobium	Nb
Cerium	Ce	Nitrogen	N
Chlorine	Cl	Nobelium	No
Chromium	Cr	Osmium	Os
Cobalt	Co	Oxygen	O
Copper (Cuprum)	Cu	Palladium	Pd
Curium	Cm	Phosphorus	P
Dysprosium	Dy	Platinum	Pt
Einsteinium	Es	Plutonium	Pu
Erbium	Er	Polonium	Po
Europium	Eu	Potassium (Kalium)	K
Fermium	Fm	Praseodymium	Pr
Fluorine	F	Promethium	Pm
Francium	Fr	Protactinium	Pa
Gadolinium	Gd	Radium	Ra
Gallium	Ga	Radon	Rn
Germanium	Ge	Rhenium	Re
Gold (Aurum)	Au	Rhodium	Rh
Hafnium	Hf	Rubidium	Rb
Hahnium	Ha	Ruthenium	Ru
Helium	He	Rutherfordium	Rf
Holmium	Ho	Samarium	Sm
Hydrogen	H	Scandium	Sc
Indium	In	Selenium	Se
Iodine	I	Silicon	Si

Name	Symbol	Name	Symbol
Silver (Argentum)	Ag	Tin (Stannum)	Sn
Sodium (Natrium)	Na	Titanium	Ti
Strontium	Sr	Tungsten (Wolfram)	W
Sulphur	S	Uranium	U
Tantalum	Ta	Vanadium	V
Technetium	Tc	Xenon	Xe
Tellurium	Te	Ytterbium	Yb
Terbium	Tb	Yttrium	Y
Thallium	Tl	Zinc	Zn
Thorium	Th	Zirconium	Zr
Thulium	Tm		

F

FRACTIONS. Do not mingle fractions with decimals. If you need to convert one to the other, use this table.See also FIGURES, page 29.

Fraction	Decimal equivalent
$1/2$	0.5
$1/3$	0.333
$1/4$	0.25
$1/5$	0.2
$1/6$	0.167
$1/7$	0.143
$1/8$	0.125
$1/9$	0.111
$1/10$	0.1
$1/11$	0.091
$1/12$	0.083
$1/13$	0.077
$1/14$	0.071
$1/15$	0.067
$1/16$	0.063
$1/17$	0.059
$1/18$	0.056
$1/19$	0.053
$1/20$	0.05

G

GEOLOGICAL ERAS. Astronomers and geologists give this broad outline of the ages of the universe and the earth.

Era, period and epoch		Years ago m	Characteristics
Origin of the universe (estimates vary markedly)		20,000 to 10,000	
Origin of the sun		5,000	
Origin of the earth		4,600	
Pre-Cambrian			
Archean		4,000	First signs of fossilised microbes
Proterozoic		2,500	
Palaeozoic			
Cambrian		570	First appearance of abundant fossils
Ordovician (obsolete)		500	Vertebrates emerge
Silurian		440	Fishes emerge
Devonian		400	Primitive plants emerge
Carboniferous		350	Amphibians emerge
Permian		270	Reptiles emerge
Mesozoic			
Triassic		250	Seed plants emerge
Jurassic		210	Age of dinosaurs
Cretaceous		145	Flowering plants emerge; dinosaurs extinct at end of this period
Cenozoic			
Palaeocene		65	
Tertiary:	Eocene	55	Mammals emerge
	Oligocene	40	
	Miocene	25	
	Pliocene	5	
Quaternary:	Pleistocene	2	Ice ages; stone age man emerges
	Holocene or Recent	10,000[a]	Modern man emerges

[a] 10,000 years, not 10,000m years.

L

LATIN.
Here are some common Latin words and phrases and their translations.

ab initio   from the beginning
ad hoc   for this object or purpose (implied and "this one only");
   therefore, without a system, spontaneously
ad hominem   to an individual's interests or passions; used of an
   argument that takes advantage of the character of the person on
   the other side
ad infinitum   to infinity, that is, endlessly
ad lib.   ad libitum, meaning at pleasure. Used adverbially or even
   as a verb when it means to invent or extemporise
ad valorem   according to value (as opposed to volume)
a fortiori   with stronger reason
annus mirabilis   wonderful year, used to describe a special year,
   one in which more than one memorable thing has happened; for
   instance 1666, the year of the Great Fire of London and the
   English defeats of the Dutch
a priori   from cause to effect, that is, deductively or from prior
   principle
cave   "Watch out!" (imperative); once used at boys' schools
caveat emptor   let the buyer beware
ceteris paribus   other things being equal
cf   short for *confer*, meaning compare
circa   around or about: used for dates and large quantities; can be
   abbreviated to *c* or *c.*
de facto   in point of fact
de jure   from the law; by right
de profundis   from the depths
deus ex machina   God from a machine; first used of a Greek
   theatrical convention, where a god would swing on to the stage,
   high up in a machine, solving humanly insoluble problems and
   thus resolving the action of a play. Now used to describe a wholly
   outside person who puts matters right.
eg   exempli gratia, for example
et al.   et alii, and others, used as an abbreviation in bibliographies
   when citing multiple editorship or authorship to save the writer
   the bother of writing out all the names. Thus, A. Bloggs *et al.,*
   The Occurrence of Endangered Species in the Genus Orthodoptera
ex cathedra   from the chair of office, authoritatively

ex officio   by virtue of one's office, not unofficially

ex parte   from or for one side only

ibid.   *ibidem*, in the same place; used in footnotes in academic works to mean that the quote comes from the same place, book, etc

idem   the same, that is mentioned before; like *ibidem*

ie   *id est*, that is, explains the material immediately in front of it

in absentia   in the absence of, used as "absent"

in camera   in a (private) room, that is, not in public

in re   in the matter of

in situ   in (its) original place

inter alia/inter alios   among other things or people

ipso facto   by that very fact, in the fact itself

loc. cit.   *loco citato*, in the place cited; used in footnotes to mean that the source of the reference or quote has already been given

mea culpa   my fault

mirabile dictu   literally, wonderful to relate

mutatis mutandis   after making the necessary changes

nem. con.   *nemine contradicente*, no one against; unanimously

op. cit.   *opere citato*, in the work quoted; similar to *loc. cit.* (q.v.)

pace   despite

pari passu   on the same terms, at an equal pace or rate of progress

passim   adverb, here and there or scattered. Used in indexes to indicate that the item is scattered throughout the work and there are too many instances to enumerate them all

persona non grata   person not in favour

petitio elenchis   the sin of assuming a conclusion

post eventum   after the event

post hoc, ergo, propter hoc   after this, therefore because of this. Used fallaciously in argument to show that because something comes after something it can be inferred that the first thing caused the second thing

post mortem   after death, used as an adjective and also as a noun, a clinical examination of a dead body

prima facie   at first sight, meaning apparently and having no connection with love

primus inter pares   first among equals

pro tem.   *pro tempore*, for the moment

PS   *post scriptum*, written afterwards

quid pro quo   something for something (or one thing for another), something in return, an equivalent; usually given

q.v.   *quod vide*, which see; means that the reader should look for the word just mentioned (eg in glossary)

re   with regard to, in the matter of

sic   thus; used in brackets in quotes to show writer has made a mistake. "Mrs Thacher (sic) resigned today."

sine die   without (setting) a date

status quo ante the same state as before; shortened to *status quo*. A common usage is "maintaining the status quo"

stet let it stand or do not delete; cancels an alteration in proofreading; dots are placed under what is to remain

sub judice under judgment or consideration; not yet decided

sub rosa under the rose, privately or furtively; not the same as under the gooseberry bush

ultra vires beyond (one's) legal power

vade mecum a little book or something carried about on the person; literally "Go with me"

versus shortened to *v* or *v.*, against; used in legal cases and games

Laws.

Scientific, economic, facetious and fatalistic laws in common use are listed here.

Boyle's Law. The pressure of a gas varies inversely with its volume at constant temperature.

Gresham's Law. When money of a high intrinsic value is in circulation with money of lesser value, it is the inferior currency which tends to remain in circulation, while the other is either hoarded or exported. In other words: "Bad money drives out good".

Grimm's Law. (Concerns mutations of the consonants in the various Germanic languages.) Proto-Indo-European voiced aspirated stops, voiced unaspirated stops and voiceless stops become respectively voiced unaspirated stops, voiceless stops and voiceless fricatives.

Heisenberg's Uncertainty Principle. Energy and time or position and momentum cannot both be accurately measured simultaneously. The product of their uncertainties is h (Planck's constant).

Hooke's Law. The stress imposed on a solid is directly proportional to the strain produced within the elastic limit.

Mendel's Principles. The Law of Segregation is that every somatic cell of an individual carries a pair of hereditary units for each character: the pairs separate during meiosis so that each gamete carries one unit only of each pair.

The Law of Independent Assortment is that the separation of units of each pair is not influenced by that of any other pair.

Murphy's Law. Anything that can go wrong will go wrong.

Ohm's Law. Electric current is directly proportional to electromotive force and inversely proportional to resistance.

Parkinson's Law. First published in *The Economist*, November 19th 1955. The author, C. Northcote Parkinson, sought to expand on the "commonplace observation that work expands so as to fill the time available for its completion". After studying Admiralty staffing levels, he concluded that in any public administrative department not actually at war the staff increase may be expected to follow this formula:

$$x = \frac{2k^m + p}{n}$$

Where k is the number of staff seeking promotion through the appointment of subordinates; p represents the difference between the ages of appointment and retirement; m is the number of hours devoted to answering minutes within the department; and n is the number of effective units being administered. Then x will be the number of new staff required each year.

Mathematicians will, of course, realise that to find the percentage increase they must multiply x by 100 and divide by the total of the previous year, thus:

$$\frac{100(2k^m + p)}{yn} \ \%$$

where y represents the total original staff. And this figure will invariably prove to be between 5.17% and 6.56%, irrespective of any variation in the amount of work (if any) to be done.

The Peter Principle. All members of a hierarchy rise to their own level of incompetence.

Say's Law of Markets. A supply of goods generates a demand for the goods.

Laws of Thermodynamics
1. The change in the internal energy of a system equals the sum of the heat added to the system and the work done on it.
2. Heat cannot be transferred from a colder to a hotter body within a system without net changes occurring in other bodies in the system.
3. It is impossible to reduce the temperature of a system to absolute zero in a finite number of steps.

Utz's Laws of Computer Programming. Any given program, when running, is obsolete. If a program is useful, it will have to be changed. Any given program will expand to fill all available memory.

Wolfe's Law of Journalism. You cannot hope/to bribe or twist,/ thank God! the/British journalist./But seeing what/the man will do/ unbribed, there's/no occasion to.

M

Measures

Rough conversions. For British, American and metric (SI) measures. Metric units not generally recommended as SI units or for use with SI are marked with an asterisk (eg Calorie*).

Acceleration

Standard gravity	=	10 metres per second squared
	=	32 feet per second squared

Area

1 square inch	=	6½ square centimetres
2 square inches	=	13 square centimetres
10¾ square feet	=	1 square metre
43 square feet	=	4 square metres
6 square yards	=	5 square metres
2½ acres	=	1 hectare
5 acres	=	2 hectares
250 acres	=	1 square kilometre
3 square miles	=	8 square kilometres

Density and concentration

4 ounces per UK gallon	=	25 grams per litre
2 ounces per US gallon	=	15 grams per litre
1 pound per cubic foot	=	16 kilograms per cubic metre
62½ pounds per cubic foot	=	1 kilogram per litre
	=	density of 1

Energy

18 British thermal units	=	19 kilojoules
4 British thermal units	=	1 kilocalorie*
1 kilocalorie* ("Calorie"*)	=	4 kilojoules

Force

7¼ poundals	=	1 newton
1 pound-force	=	4½ newtons
1 pounds-force	=	40 newtons
1 kilogram-force	=	10 newtons

Fuel consumption

5 UK gallons per mile	=	14 litres per kilometre
20 miles per UK gallon	=	7 kilometres per litre
20 miles per UK gallon	=	14 litres per 100 kilometres
5 miles per US gallon	=	6 miles per UK gallon

Length

Width of thumb	=	1 inch
	=	25 millimetres
1 inch	=	2½ centimetres
2 inches	=	5 centimetres
1 foot	=	30 centimetres
	=	0.3 metre
3¼ feet	=	1 metre
39 inches	=	1 metre
11 yards	=	10 metres
⅝ mile	=	1 kilometre
5 miles	=	8 kilometres
8 miles	=	7 nautical miles (international)

Power

4 UK horsepower	=	3 kilowatts
72 UK horsepower	=	73 metric horsepower*

Pressure and stress

1 pound-force per square foot	=	48 pascals (newtons per square metre)
1 pound-force per square inch	=	7 kilopascals (kilonewtons per square metre)
1 bar	=	1 standard atmosphere
	=	14½ pounds-force per square inch
100 pounds-force per square inch	=	7 kilograms-force per square centimetre

Velocity (speed)

2 miles per hour	=	3 feet per second
9 miles per hour	=	4 metres per second
8 kilometres per hour	=	5 metres per second
11 kilometres per hour	=	10 feet per second
30 miles per hour	=	48 kilometres per hour
50 miles per hour	=	80 kilometres per hour
70 miles per hour	=	113 kilometres per hou

Volume and capacity

1 teaspoonful	=	5 millilitres
1 UK fluid ounce	=	28 millilitres
26 UK fluid ounces	=	25 US liquid ounces
3 cubic inches	=	49 cubic centimetres
	=	49 millilitres
1¾ UK pints	=	1 litre
7 UK pints	=	4 litres
7 UK quarts	=	8 litres
5 UK pints	=	6 US liquid pints
9 US liquid pints	=	9 litres
1 UK gallon	=	4½ litres
2 UK gallons	=	9 litres

$$5 \text{ UK gallons} = 6 \text{ US gallons}$$
$$1 \text{ US gallon} = 3\tfrac{3}{4} \text{ litres}$$
$$4 \text{ US gallons} = 15 \text{ litres}$$
$$3 \text{ cubic feet} = 85 \text{ cubic decimetres}$$
$$= 85 \text{ litres}$$
$$35 \text{ cubic feet} = 1 \text{ cubic metre}$$
$$4 \text{ cubic yards} = 3 \text{ cubic metres}$$
$$31 \text{ UK bushels} = 32 \text{ US bushels}$$
$$27\tfrac{1}{2} \text{ UK bushels} = 1 \text{ cubic metre}$$
$$28\tfrac{1}{3} \text{ US bushels} = 1 \text{ cubic metre}$$
$$11 \text{ UK bushels} = 4 \text{ hectolitres}$$
$$14 \text{ US bushels} = 5 \text{ hectolitres}$$
$$1 \text{ US bushel (heaped)} = 1\tfrac{1}{4} \text{ US bushels (struck)}$$
$$1 \text{ US dry barrel} = 3\tfrac{1}{4} \text{ US bushels}$$
$$1 \text{ US cranberry barrel} = 2\tfrac{3}{4} \text{ bushels}$$
$$1 \text{ barrel (petroleum)} = 42 \text{ US gallons}$$
$$= 35 \text{ UK gallons}$$
$$1 \text{ barrel per day} = 50 \text{ tonnes per year}$$

Weight

$$1 \text{ grain} = 65 \text{ milligrams}$$
$$15 \text{ grains} = 1 \text{ gram}$$
$$11 \text{ ounces} = 10 \text{ ounces troy}$$
$$1 \text{ ounce} = 28 \text{ grams}$$
$$1 \text{ ounce troy} = 31 \text{ grams}$$
$$1 \text{ pound} = 454 \text{ grams}$$
$$5 \text{ ounces} = 1 \text{ kilogram}$$
$$2\tfrac{1}{4} \text{ pounds} = 1 \text{ kilogram}$$
$$11 \text{ stones} = 70 \text{ kilograms}$$
$$11 \text{ US hundredweights} = 5 \text{ quintals}^\star$$
$$2 \text{ UK hundredweights} = 1 \text{ quintal}^\star$$
$$2{,}205 \text{ pounds} = 1 \text{ tonne}$$
$$11 \text{ US tons} = 10 \text{ tonnes}$$
$$62 \text{ UK tons} = 63 \text{ tonnes}$$
$$100 \text{ UK (long) tons} = 112 \text{ US (short) tons}$$

Yield

$$3 \text{ UK or US bushels per acre} = 2 \text{ quintals}^\star \text{ per hectare}$$
$$10 \text{ UK or US bushels per acre} = 9 \text{ hectolitres per hectare}$$
$$1 \text{ UK hundredweight per acre} = 1\tfrac{1}{4} \text{ quintals}^\star \text{ per hectare}$$
$$1 \text{ UK ton per acre} = 2\tfrac{1}{2} \text{ tonnes per hectare}$$
$$9 \text{ pounds per acre} = 10 \text{ kilograms per hectare}$$

METRIC SYSTEM PREFIXES.

Prefix name & symbol		Factor by which unit is multiplied	Description
atto	a	10^{-18}= 0.000 000 000 000 000 001	
femto	f	10^{-15}= 0.000 000 000 000 001	
pico	p	10^{-12}= 0.000 000 000 001	million millionth; trillionth
nano	n	10^{-9} = 0.000 000 001	thousand millionth; billionth
micro	μ	10^{-6} = 0.000 001	millionth
milli	m	10^{-3} = 0.001	thousandth
centi	c	10^{-2} = 0.01	hundredth
deci	d	10^{-1} = 0.1	tenth

Prefix name & symbol		Factor by which unit is multiplied	Description
deca (or deka)	da[a]	10^{1} = 10	ten
hecto	h	10^{2} = 100	hundred
kilo	k	10^{3} = 1,000	thousand
myria	my	10^{4} = 10,000	ten thousand
mega	M	10^{6} = 1,000,000	million
giga	G	10^{9} = 1,000,000,000	thousand million; billion
tera	T	10^{12} = 1,000,000,000,000	million million; trillion
peta	P	10^{15} = 1,000,000,000,000,000	
exa	E	10^{18} = 1,000,000,000,000,000,000	

[a] Sometimes dk is used (eg in Germany).

UNITS WITH DIFFERENT EQUIVALENTS.
Barrel

UK (beer)	=	36 UK gallons
	=	164 litres
USA: dry standard	=	7,056 cubic inches
	=	116 litres
petroleum	=	42 US gallons
	=	159 litres
standard cranberry	=	5,826 cubic inches
	=	95.5 litres
various (liquid)	=	31–42 US gallons
	=	117–151 litres

Bushel

UK	=	2,219.36 cubic inches
	=	36.37 litres
Old English, Winchester ⎫		
USA[a] (struck[b]) ⎭	=	2,150 42 cubic inches
	=	35.24 litres
USA (heaped)	=	2,747 715 cubic inches
	=	45.03 litres

[a]   The most usual unit.
[b]   Levelled off at the top.
[c]   Used for apples.

Centner or Zentner

UK	=	cental of 100 pounds
	=	45.36 kilograms
Commercial hundredweight in several European countries, generally 50 kilograms	=	110.23 pounds
Metric centner of 100 kilograms	=	220.46 pounds

Chain

UK: Gunter's/surveyors'	=	66 feet
	=	20.12 metres}
Engineers'	=	100 feet
	=	30.48 metres

Foot

UK ⎫		
USA customary ⎭	=	12 inches
	=	0.304 8 metre
USA survey	=	12.000 02 inches
	=	0.304 800 6 metre
Canada: Paris foot	=	12.789 inches
	=	0.325 metre
Cape foot	=	12.396 inches
	=	0.315 metre
Chinese foot (*che* or *chih*):		
old system	=	14.1 inches
	=	0.358 metre
new system	=	13.123 inches
	=	0.333 33 metre

Gallon

UK	=	277.42 cubic inches
	=	4.546 litres
Old English, Winchester, Wine ⎫		
USA, liquid ⎭	=	231 cubic inches
	=	3.785 litres
USA, dry	=	268.802 5 cubic inches
	=	0.004 4 cubic metre

Gill

UK	=	8.669 cubic inches
	=	142.1 millilitres
USA	=	7.218 75 cubic inches
	=	118.3 millilitres

Hundredweight

UK ⎫		
USA, long ⎭	=	112 pounds
	=	50.8 kilograms
USA, short	=	100 pounds
	=	45.4 kilograms

Link

UK: Gunter's/surveyors'	=	0.66 foot
	=	0.201 2 metre
Engineers'	=	1 foot
	=	0.304 8 metre

Mile

UK: imperial	=	5,280 feet
	=	1.609 344 kilometres
geographical	=	6,080 feet
	=	1.853 184 kilometres[a]
nautical		
sea		
USA	=	5,280 feet
	=	1.609 344 kilometres
International nautical	=	1,852 metres
	=	6,076.12 feet

[a] In practice sometimes 6,000 feet = 1.8288 kilometres

Ounce

Dry: ounce	=	437½ grains
	=	28.35 grams
ounce troy	=	480 grains
	=	31.01 grams
Liquid or fluid ounce: UK	=	1.734 cubic inches
	=	28.4 millilitres
USA	=	1.805 cubic inches
	=	29.6 millilitres

[a] 20 fluid ounces = 1 pint
[b] 16 liquid ounces = 1 liquid pint

Peck

UK	=	554.839 cubic inches
	=	9.092 cubic decimetres (litres)
USA	=	537.605 cubic inches
	=	8.810 cubic decimetres (litres)

Pint

UK	=	34.677 4 cubic inches
	=	0.568 litre

USA: dry	=	33.600 312 5 cubic inches
	=	0.551 cubic decimetre (litre)
liquid	=	28.875 cubic inches
	=	0.473 litre

Pound

UK ⎫
USA ⎭

avoirdupois pound	=	0.454 kilogram
USA: troy pound	=	0.373 kilogram
	=	0.823 pound (avoirdupois)
Spanish (libra)	=	0.460 kilogram
	=	1.014 pounds (avoirdupois)
"Amsterdam"	=	0.494 kilogram
	=	1.089 pounds (avoirdupois)
Danish (pund)	=	0.5 kilogram
	=	1.102 pounds (avoirdupois)
Française (livre)	=	0.490 kilogram
	=	1.079 pounds (avoirdupois)

Quart

UK	=	69.355 cubic inches
	=	1.137 litres
USA: dry	=	67.200 625 cubic inches
	=	1.101 cubic decimetres (litres)
liquid	=	57.75 cubic inches
	=	0.946 litre

Quarter

UK: capacity	=	8 bushels
	=	64 gallons
	=	2.909 hectolitres
	=	0.290 9 cubic metre
weight (mass)	=	28 pounds
	=	12.701 kilograms
cloth	=	9 inches
	=	22.86 centimetres
wines and spirits	=	27½–30 gallons
	=	125–136 litres

Quintal

Hundredweight: UK	=	112 pounds
	=	50.8 kilograms
USA	=	100 pounds
	=	45.4 kilograms
Metric quintal	=	100 kilograms
	=	220.46 pounds
Spanish quintal	=	46 kilograms
	=	101.4 pounds

Stone

UK: Imperial	=	14 pounds
	=	6.350 kilograms

121

Smithfield	=	8 pounds
	=	3.629 kilograms

Ton

UK: weight (mass)	=	2,240 pounds
	=	1.016 tonnes
shipping: register	=	100 cubic feet
	=	2.832 cubic metres
USA: short	=	2,000 pounds
	=	0.907 tonne
long	=	2,240 pounds
	=	1.016 tonnes
Metric ton (tonne)	=	1,000 kilograms
	=	2,204.62 pounds
Spanish:short (corta)	=	2,000 libras
	=	0.920 2 tonne
	=	2,028.7 pounds
long (larga)	=	2,240 libras
	=	1.030 6 tonnes
	=	2,272.1 pounds

See also MEASUREMENTS, page 41.

N

NATIONAL ACCOUNTS.
These are the definitions adopted by the United Nations in 1968.

Final expenditure
- = private final consumption expenditure ("consumers' expenditure")
- + government final consumption expenditure
- + increase in stocks
- + gross fixed capital formation
- + exports of goods and services

Gross domestic product (GDP) at market prices
- = final expenditure
- - imports of goods and services

Gross national product (GNP) at market prices
- = gross domestic product at market prices
- + net property income from other countries

Gross domestic product at factor cost
- = gross domestic product at market prices
- - indirect taxes
- + subsidies

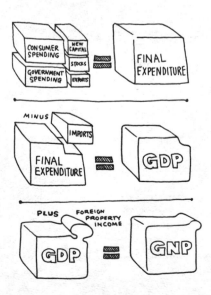

O

OLYMPIC GAMES.

I	Athens	1896	XIII	London (cancelled)	1944
II	Paris	1900	XIV	London	1948
III	St Louis	1904	XV	Helsinki	1952
	Athens	1906	XVI	Melbourne	1956
IV	London	1908	XVII	Rome	1960
V	Stockholm	1912	XVIII	Tokyo	1964
VI	Berlin (cancelled)	1916	XIX	Mexico City	1968
VII	Antwerp	1920	XX	Munich	1972
VIII	Paris	1924	XXI	Montreal	1976
IX	Amsterdam	1928	XXII	Moscow	1980
X	Los Angeles	1932	XXIII	Los Angeles	1984
XI	Berlin	1936	XXIV	Seoul	1988
XII	Tokyo/Helsinki	1940	XXV	Barcelona	1992
	(cancelled)		XXVI	Atlanta	1996

ORGANISATIONS

These are the exact names and abbreviated titles of the main international organisations. Where membership is small or exclusive, members are listed too.

ALADI. Latin American Integration Association.
Members

Argentina	Colombia[a]	Peru[a]
Bolivia[a]	Ecuador[a]	Uruguay
Brazil	Mexico	Venezuela[a]
Chile	Paraguay	

a These countries are also members of the Andean Group.

ASEAN. Association of South East Asian Nations.
Members

Brunei	Philippines	Vietnam
Indonesia	Singapore	
Malaysia	Thailand	

BIS. Bank for International Settlements. The central bankers' central bank, in Basle.

Members

Australia	Greece	Portugal
Austria	Hungary	Romania
Belgium	Iceland	Slovakia
Bulgaria	Ireland	South Africa
Canada	Italy	Spain
Czech Republic	Japan	Sweden
Denmark	Latvia	Switzerland
Estonia	Lithuania	Turkey
Finland	Netherlands	United Kingdom
France	Norway	United States of
Germany	Poland	America

CARICOM. Caribbean Community and Common Market.
Members

Antigua and Barbuda	Jamaica
Bahamas	Montserrat
Barbados	St Kitts-Nevis
Belize	St Lucia
British Virgin Islands[a]	St Vincent and the Grenadines
Dominica	Trinidad and Tobago
Grenada	Turks and Caicos Islands[a]
Guyana	

a Associate members.

COMECON. The Council for Mutual Economic Assistance, which was the communist world's version of what has now become the European Union; dissolved 1991.
Members

Bulgaria	Hungary	Romania
Czechoslovakia	Mongolia	Soviet Union
Cuba	Poland	Vietnam
East Germany		

COMMONWEALTH.

Members	Cyprus	Malawi
Antigua and	Dominica	Malaysia
Barbuda	The Gambia	Maldives
Australia	Ghana	Malta
Bahamas	Grenada	Mauritius
Bangladesh	Guyana	Namibia
Barbados	India	Nauru[a]
Belize	Jamaica	New Zealand
Botswana	Kenya	Nigeria
Brunei	Kiribati	Pakistan[b]
Canada	Lesotho	Papua New Guinea

PART III

St Kitts-Nevis   South Africa[b]   Uganda
St Lucia   Sri Lanka   United Kingdom
St Vincent and the   Swaziland   Vanuatu
  Grenadines   Tanzania   Western Samoa
Seychelles   Tonga   Zambia
Sierra Leone   Trinidad and   Zimbabwe
Singapore   Tobago
Solomon Islands   Tuvalu[a]

a Does not attend Commonwealth summits.
b Pakistan withdrew in 1972, but rejoined in 1989. South Africa withdrew in 1961,
  but rejoined in 1994. Fiji's membership lapsed in 1987 after the proclamation of a
  republic.

Dependencies and associated states
Australia:
Ashmore and Cartier Islands   Coral Sea Islands Territory
Australian Antarctic Territory   Heard and McDonald Islands
Christmas Island   Norfolk Island
Cocos (Keeling) Islands

New Zealand:
Cook Islands   Ross Dependency
Niue   Tokelau

United Kingdom:
Anguilla   Gibraltar
Bermuda   Hong Kong (until 1997)
British Antarctic Territory   Isle of Man
British Indian Ocean Territory   Montserrat
British Virgin Islands   Pitcairn Islands
Cayman Islands   St Helena and dependencies
Channel Islands   Ascension
Falkland Islands and dependencies Tristan da Cunha
  South Georgia   Turks and Caicos Islands
  South Sandwich Islands

COMMONWEALTH OF INDEPENDENT STATES (CIS). Founded
in December 1991 by the former Soviet Socialist Republics with the
exception of Georgia, which joined later.
Members
Armenia   Kazakhstan   Tajikistan
Azerbaijan   Kirgizstan   Turkmenistan
Belarus   Moldova   Ukraine
Georgia   Russia   Uzbekistan

See also EX-SOVIET UNION.

126

Csce. Conference on Security and Co-operation in Europe. Originally founded in 1972. 53 members.

Eu. European Union, the collective designation of three organisations with common membership. These organisations are: the European Coal and Steel Community (ECSC), European Economic Community (EEC) and European Atomic Energy Community (EURATOM). They merged to become the European Community (EC) in 1967 and in November 1993 when the Maastricht treaty came into force the EC was incorporated into the European Union.
Members

Austria	Germany[a]	Netherlands[a]
Belgium[a]	Greece	Portugal
Denmark	Ireland	Spain
Finland	Italy[a]	Sweden
France[a]	Luxembourg[a]	United Kingdom

a Founding members.

Ecowas. Economic Community of West African States.
Members

Benin	Guinea	Niger
Burkina Faso	Guinea-Bissau	Nigeria
Cape Verde	Liberia	Senegal
Côte d'Ivoire	Mali	Sierra Leone
The Gambia	Mauritania	Togo
Ghana		

Efta. European Free Trade Association.
Members

Iceland	Norway
Liechtenstein	Switzerland

Franc Zone. Comité Monétaire de la Zone Franc.
Members

Benina	Comoros[b]	Mali[a]
Burkina Faso[a]	Congo[b]	Niger
Cameroon[b]	Côte d'Ivoire[a]	Senegal[a]
Central African Republic[b]	Equatorial Guinea[b]	Togo[a]
Chad[b]	France[c]	
	Gabon[b]	

a Member of Banque Centrale des Etats de l'Afrique de l'Ouest.
b Member of Banque des Etats de l'Afrique Centrale.
c Metropolitan France, Mayotte, St Pierre and Miquelon and the Overseas Departments and Territories.

GCC. Co-operation Council for the Arab States of the Gulf. Its normal shorthand name is Gulf Co-operation Council.
Members

Bahrain	Qatar
Kuwait	Saudi Arabia
Oman	United Arab Emirates

GROUP OF SEVEN (G-7). A subset of the G-10, whose members are Canada, France, Germany, Italy, Japan, the UK and the USA. It has no organisational structure. Holds formal summit meetings of heads of state or their representatives. Although primarily a forum for discussing economic problems, the G-7 is increasingly becoming involved in politics.

GROUP OF TEN (G-10). The ten countries – Belgium, Canada, France, Germany, Italy, Japan, the Netherlands, Sweden, the UK and the USA, and an honorary eleventh member, Switzerland – that agreed to provide credit of $6 billion to the International Monetary Fund in 1962, known as the General Arrangement to Borrow. The G-10 is a convenient forum for discussing international monetary arrangements; it hatched the Smithsonian agreement and currency changes in 1971. The G-10 also meets through its central bank, the Bank for International Settlements (BIS) based in Basle.

IATA. International Air Transport Association. Head offices: Montreal and Geneva. *Members*: most international airlines.

NATO. North Atlantic Treaty Organisation.
Members

Belgium	Iceland	Portugal
Canada	Italy	Spain
Denmark	Luxembourg	Turkey
France[a]	Netherlands	United Kingdom
Germany	Norway	United States of America
Greece		

a France withdrew from the integrated military structure in 1966 but remains a member of the Atlantic Alliance.

NATO's "Partnerships for Peace" programme, launched in 1994, is aimed at getting former communist countries in eastern Europe and the former Soviet Union to take part in a wide range of military co-operation arrangements without having the full obligations or benefits of NATO membership. By the beginning of 1996 more than 20 countries had concluded "Partnership for Peace" agreements with NATO.

OAU. Organization of African Unity.
Members

Algeria	Ethiopia	Nigeria
Angola	Gabon	Rwanda
Benin	The Gambia	Senegal
Botswana	Ghana	Seychelles
Burkina Faso	Guinea	Sierra Leone
Burundi	Guinea-Bissau	Somalia
Cameroon	Kenya	South Africa
Cape Verde	Lesotho	Sudan
Central African	Liberia	Swaziland
Republic	Libya	São Tomé and
Chad	Madagascar	Principe
Comoros	Malawi	Tanzania
Congo	Mali	Togo
Côte d'Ivoire	Mauritania	Tunisia
Djibouti	Mauritius	Uganda
Egypt	Mozambique	Zaire
Equatorial Guinea	Namibia	Zambia
Eritrea	Niger	Zimbabwe

The Sahara Arab Democratic Republic (Western Sahara) was admitted in February 1982, following recognition by 26 of the 50 members. Its membership was disputed by Morocco and others which claimed that a two-thirds majority was needed to admit a state whose existence is in question. Morocco withdrew from the OAU with effect from November 1985.

OAS. Organization of American States.
Members

Antigua and	Dominican	Paraguay
Barbuda	Republic	Peru
Argentina	Ecuador	St Kitts-Nevis
Bahamas	El Salvador	St Lucia
Barbados	Grenada	St Vincent and the
Bolivia	Guatemala	Grenadines
Brazil	Guyana	Suriname
Canada	Haiti	Trinidad and
Chile	Honduras	Tobago
Colombia	Jamaica	United States of
Costa Rica	Mexico	America
Cuba	Nicaragua	Uruguay
Dominica	Panama	Venezuela

OECD. Organisation for Economic Co-operation and Development. Capitalism's club, based in Paris.

Members

Australia	Iceland	Portugal
Austria	Ireland	Spain
Belgium	Italy	Sweden
Canada	Japan	Switzerland
Denmark	Luxembourg	Turkey
Finland	Mexico	United Kingdom
France	Netherlands	United States of America
Germany	New Zealand	
Greece	Norway	

The Czech Republic, Slovakia, Hungary and Poland have participated in the OECD's "Partners in transition" programme since 1991. An agreement was signed with Russia in June 1994. Ministers also agreed to start membership negotiations with the Czech Republic, Hungary, Poland, Slovakia and South Korea.

OPEC. Organization of Petroleum Exporting Countries.
Members

Algeria	Iraq	Qatar
Gabon	Kuwait	Saudi Arabia
Indonesia	Libya	United Arab Emirates
Iran	Nigeria	Venezuela

THE UNITED NATIONS. New York.

General Assembly | Trusteeship Council
Security Council | International Court of Justice
Economic and Social Council Secretariat (ECOSOC)
Main bodies

Regional Commissions of ECOSOC		*Head office*
Economic Commission for Africa	ECA	Addis Ababa
Economic Commission for Europe	ECE	Geneva
Economic and Social Commission for Asia and the Pacific	ESCAP	Bangkok
Economic Commission for Latin America and the Caribbean	ECLAC	Santiago, Chile
Economic and Social Commission for Western Asia	ESCWA	Amman

Other United Nations bodies		
International Sea-Bed Authority		Kingston, Jamaica
Office of the United Nations Disaster Relief Co-ordinator	UNDRO	Geneva
United Nations Centre for Human Settlements	UNCHS (HABITAT)	Nairobi
United Nations Children's Fund	UNICEF	New York

United Nations Conference on Trade and Development	UNCTAD	Geneva
United Nations Development Programme	UNDP	New York
United Nations Environment Programme	UNEP	Nairobi
United Nations High Commissioner for Refugees	UNHCR	Geneva
United Nations Observer Missions and Peace-keeping Forces		New York
United Nations Population Fund	UNFPA	New York
United Nations Relief and Works Agency for Palestine Refugees in the Near East	UNRWA	Vienna
World Food Council	WFC	Rome
World Food Programme	WFP	Rome

Specialised agencies within the UN system

Food and Agriculture Organization	FAO	Rome
General Agreement on Tariffs and Trade	GATT	Geneva
International Atomic Energy Agency	IAEA	Vienna
International Bank for Reconstruction and Development (World Bank)	IBRD	Washington, DC
International Civil Aviation Organization	ICAO	Montreal
International Development Association	IDA	Washington, DC
International Finance Corporation	IFC	Washington, DC
International Fund for Agricultural Development	IFAD	Rome
International Labour Organisation	ILO	Geneva
International Maritime Organization	IMO	London
International Monetary Fund	IMF	Washington, DC
International Telecommunications Union	ITU	Geneva
Multilateral Investment Guarantee Agency	MIGA	Washington, DC
United Nations Educational, Scientific and Cultural Organization	UNESCO	Paris
United Nations Industrial Development Organization	UNIDO	Vienna
Universal Postal Union	UPU	Berne
World Health Organization	WHO	Geneva
World Intellectual Property Organization	WIPO	Geneva
World Meteorological Organization	WMO	Geneva

R

ROMAN NUMERALS.

I	1	XIII	13	XC	90
II	2	XIV	14	C	100
III	3	XV	15	CC	200
IV	4	XVI	16	D	500
V	5	XVII	17	DCC	700
VI	6	XVIII	18	DCCXIX	719
VII	7	XIX	19	CM	900
VIII	8	XX	20	M	1000
IX	9	XXI	21	MC	1100
X	10	XXX	30	MCX	1110
XI	11	XL	40	MCMXCI	1991
XII	12	L	50	MM	2000

S

STATES, REGIONS, PROVINCES, COUNTIES

Here are the correct spellings of the main administrative subdivisions of industrialised countries. Accents should be used. See also COUNTRIES AND THEIR INHABITANTS.

AUSTRALIA (Commonwealth of Australia)

States
New South Wales
Queensland
South Australia
Tasmania
Victoria
Western Australia

Territories
Australian Capital Territory
Northern Territory

BELGIUM (Kingdom of Belgium)

Provinces
Antwerp (Anvers)
Brabant
East Flanders (Oost-Vlaanderen)
Hainaut
Liège

Limburg
Luxembourg
Namur
West Flanders
    (West-Vlaanderen)

BRAZIL (Federal Republic of Brazil)

States
Acre
Alagoas
Amapá
Amazonas
Bahia
Ceará
Espírito Santo
Goiás
Maranhão
Mato Grosso
Mato Grosso do Sul
Minas Gerais
Pará
Paraíba

Paraná
Pernambuco
Piauí
Rio de Janeiro
Rio Grande do Norte
Rio Grande do Sul
Rondônia
Roraima
Santa Catarina
São Paulo
Sergipe
Tocantins
Distrito Federal
    (Federal District, Brasília)

CANADA
Provinces

Alberta	Prince Edward Island
British Columbia	Quebec (Québec)
Manitoba	Saskatchewan
New Brunswick	
Newfoundland	*Territories*
Nova Scotia	Northwest Territories
Ontario	Yukon Territory

FRANCE (Republic of France)
Regions

Alsace	Ile-de-France
Aquitaine	Languedoc-Roussillon
Auvergne	Limousin
Basse Normandie	Lorraine
Brittany (Bretagne)	Midi-Pyrénées
Burgundy (Bourgogne)	Nord Pas-de-Calais
Centre	Pays de la Loire
Champagne-Ardenne	Picardy (Picardie)
Corsica (Corse)	Poitou-Charentes
Franche Comté	Provence Alpes Côte d'Azur
Haute Normandie	Rhône-Alpes

GERMANY (Federal Republic of Germany)
States (in German *Länder*)

Berlin[a]	North Rhine-Westphalia
Baden-Württemberg	(Nordrhein-Westfalen)
Bavaria (Bayern)	Rhineland-Palatinate
Brandenburg[b]	(Rheinland-Pfalz)
Bremen	Saarland
Hamburg	Saxony (Sachsen)[b]
Hesse (Hessen)	Saxony-Anhalt (Sachsen-
Lower Saxony (Niedersachsen)	Anhalt)[b]
Thuringia (Thüringen)[b]	Schleswig-Holstein
Mecklenburg-Vorpommern[b]	

a Formerly West Berlin.
b Former East German states.

IRELAND (Republic of Ireland)

Provinces	*Counties*	
Connacht	Galway	Roscommon
	Leitrim	Sligo
	Mayo	
Leinster	Carlow	Kildare
	Dublin	Kilkenny

	Laois	Offaly
	Longford	Westmeath
	Louth	Wexford
	Meath	Wicklow
Munster	Clare	Limerick
	Cork	Tipperary
	Kerry	Waterford
Ulster	Cavan	Monaghan
	Donegal	

ITALY (Italian Republic)
Regions

Abruzzi
Basilicata
Calabria
Campania
Emilia-Romagna
Friuli-Venezia Giulia
Lazio
Liguria
Lombardy (Lombardia)
Marche

Molise
Piedmont (Piemonte)
Puglia
Sardinia (Sardegna)
Sicily (Sicilia)
Tuscany (Toscana)
Trentino-Alto Adige
Umbria
Valle d'Aosta
Veneto

NETHERLANDS (Kingdom of the Netherlands)
Provinces

Drente
Flevoland
Friesland
Gelderland
Groningen
Limburg

Noord Brabant
Noord Holland
Overijssel
Utrecht
Zeeland
Zuid-Holland

EX-SOVIET UNION (Union of Soviet Socialist Republics)
The former Soviet Union has broken up. The three Baltic republics
– Estonia, Latvia and Lithuania – have become independent coun-
tries. The other republics are independent members of the COM-
MONWEALTH OF INDEPENDENT STATES. The former autonomous
Soviet socialist republics are no longer Soviet or even socialist, but
they, and the autonomous regions, have mostly retained their status.
Former Soviet Socialist Republics

Armenian (Armenia)
Azerbaijan
Belorussian (Belarus)
Georgian (Georgia)
Kazakh (Kazakhstan)
Kirgiz (Kirgizstan)

Moldavian (Moldova)
Russian SFSR (Russia)
Tajik (Tajikistan)
Turkmen ((Turkmenistan)
Ukrainian (Ukraine)
Uzbek (Uzbekistan)

Former Autonomous Soviet Socialist Republics
Within **Russia**:

Bashkir	Komi
Buryat	Mari
Chechen	Mordovian
Chuvash	North Ossetian
Dagestan	Tatar
Ingush	Tuva
Kabardino-Balkar	Udmurt
Kalmyk	Yakut

Within Azerbaijan: Nakhichevan
Within Georgia: Abkhazia, Adzhar
Within Uzbekistan: Karakalpak

Autonomous Regions
Within Russia: Adygei, Gorno-Altai, Jewish,
    Karachai-Cherkess, Khakass
Within Azerbaijan: Nagorno-Karabakh
Within Georgia: South Ossetian
Within Tajikistan: Gorno-Badakhshan

SPAIN
Autonomous Communities

Andalucía	Catalonia (Cataluña)
Aragón	Extremadura
Asturias	Galicia
Balearic Islands (Baleares)	Madrid
Basque Country (Euskadi)	Murcia
Canary Islands (Canarias)	Navarra
Cantabria	Rioja
Castilla Y León	Valencia
Castilla-La Mancha	

UNITED KINGDOM
England: Counties

Avon	Devon	Hertfordshire
Bedfordshire	Dorset	Humberside
Berkshire	Durham	Isle of Wight
Buckinghamshire	East Sussex	Kent
Cambridgeshire	Essex	Lancashire
Cheshire	Gloucestershire	Leicestershire
Cleveland	Greater London[a]	Lincolnshire
Cornwall/Isles of Scilly	Greater Manchester[a]	Merseyside[a]
Cumbria	Hampshire	Norfolk
Derbyshire	Hereford and Worcester	North Yorkshire
		Northamptonshire

Northumberland   South Yorkshire[a]   Warwickshire
Nottinghamshire   Staffordshire   West Midlands[a]
Oxfordshire   Suffolk   West Sussex
Shropshire   Surrey   West Yorkshire[a]
Somerset   Tyne & Wear[a]   Wiltshire

a Created in 1974 when local government was reorganised. Their councils were abolished in 1986.

Wales: *Counties*
Clwyd   Gwynedd   South Glamorgan
Dyfed   Mid Glamorgan   West Glamorgan
Gwent   Powys

Scotland: *Regions*
Borders   Grampian   Strathclyde
Central   Highland   Tayside
Dumfries and   Lothian   Western Isles
   Galloway   Orkney
Fife   Shetland

Northern Ireland: *Districts*
Antrim   Coleraine   Londonderry
Ards   Cookstown   Magherafelt
Armagh   Craigavon   Moyle
Ballymena   Down   Newry and Mourne
Ballymoney   Dungannon   Newtownabbey
Banbridge   Fermanagh   North Down
Belfast   Larne   Omagh
Carrickfergus   Limavady   Strabane
Castlereagh   Lisburn

UNITED STATES OF AMERICA
States
Alabama   Idaho   Missouri
Alaska   Illinois   Montana
Arizona   Indiana   Nebraska
Arkansas   Iowa   Nevada
California   Kansas   New Hampshire
Colorado   Kentucky   New Jersey
Connecticut   Louisiana   New Mexico
Delaware   Maine   New York
Federal District of   Maryland   North Carolina
   Columbia (DC)[a]   Massachusetts   North Dakota
Florida   Michigan   Ohio
Georgia   Minnesota   Oklahoma
Hawaii   Mississippi   Oregon

Pennsylvania	Texas	West Virginia
Rhode Island	Utah	Wisconsin
South Carolina	Vermont	Wyoming
South Dakota	Virginia	
Tennessee	Washington	[a] DC is not a state.

YUGOSLAVIA

By 1992 it was clear that the break-up of the federal republic was beyond doubt. It had been made up of the following republics and autonomous provinces. The rump of Yugoslavia now comprises the republics of Serbia and Montenegro.

Republics

Bosnia and Herzegovina
  (Bosnia-Hercegovina)[a]
Croatia (Hrvatska)[a]
Macedonia (Makedonija)[a]

Montenegro (Crna Gora)
Serbia (Srbija)
Slovenia (Slovenija)[a]

a Now internationally recognised independent countries.

Autonomous Provinces
Within Serbia: Vojvodina, Kosovo

STOCK MARKET INDICES.

December 1995. These lists are frequently changed. Most of these COMPANIES are public limited companies (PLCs).

THE FINANCIAL TIMES ORDINARY SHARE INDEX (the 30 Share Index) consists of the following.

Allied-Domecq
ASDA Group
BICC
BOC Group (The)
BTR
Blue Circle Industries
Boots Co. (The)
British Airways
British Gas
British Petroleum Company (The)
British Telecommunications
Cadbury Schweppes
Courtaulds
Forte
GKN
General Electric Company (The)

Glaxo Wellcome
Grand Metropolitan
Guinness
Hanson
Imperial Chemical Industries
Lucas Industries
Marks and Spencer
National Westminster Bank
Peninsular and Oriental Steam
  Navigation Co. (The)
Reuters Holdings
Royal Insurance Holdings
SmithKline Beecham
Tate & Lyle
Thorn EMI

THE FINANCIAL TIMES STOCK EXCHANGE 100 SHARE INDEX
consists of the following.

3i
Abbey National
Allied-Domecq
Argyll Group
Arjo Wiggins
ASDA Group
Associated British Foods
BAA
B.A.T Industries
BOC Group (The)
BTR
Bank of Scotland (The Governor
  & Company of the)
Barclays
Bass
Blue Circle Industries
Boots Co. (The)
British Aerospace
British Airways
British Gas
British Petroleum Company
  (The)
BSkyB
British Steel
British Telecommunications
Burmah Castrol
Cable and Wireless
Cadbury Schweppes
Carlton Communications
Commercial Union Assurance
  Co.
Cookson
Courtaulds
De La Rue
Enterprise Oil
Forte
GKN
General Accident Fire and Life
  Assurance Corporation
General Electric Company (The)
Glaxo Wellcome
Granada Group
Grand Metropolitan
Great Universal Stores (The)
Guinness

HSBC Holdings
Hanson
Imperial Chemical Industries
Inchcape
Kingfisher
LASMO
Ladbroke Group
Land Securities
Legal & General Group
Lloyds Bank
London Electricity
Marks and Spencer
Midlands Electricity
National Westminster Bank
National Power
North West Water Group
Pearson
Peninsular and Oriental Steam
  Navigation Company (The)
PowerGen
Prudential Corporation
REXAM
RMC
RTZ Corporation (The)
Rank Organisation (The)
Reckitt & Colman
Redland
Reed International
Rentokil Group
Reuters Holdings
Rolls Royce
Royal Bank of Scotland (The)
Royal Insurance Holdings
Sainsbury (J)
Schroders
Scottish & Newcastle Breweries
ScottishPower
Sears
Severn Trent
'Shell' Transport and Trading Co
Siebe
Smith & Nephew
SmithKline Beecham
SmithKline Beecham Utilities
Southern Electric

139

Standard Chartered
Sun Alliance Group
TI Group
TSB Group
Tate & Lyle
Tesco
Thames Water
Thorn EMI

Tomkins
Unilever
Vodafone Group
Whitbread & Company
Williams Holdings
Wolseley
Zeneca

THE DOW JONES INDUSTRIAL AVERAGE consists of the following companies.

Allied-Signal
Aluminum Co. of America (ALCOA)
American Express Co.
American Telephone & Telegraph Co.
Bethlehem Steel Corp.
Boeing Company (The)
Caterpillar
Chevron Corp.
Coca-Cola Co. (The)
Walt Disney
E.I. Du Pont de Nemours & Co.
Eastman Kodak Co.
Exxon Corp.
General Electric Co.
General Motors Corp.
Goodyear Tire & Rubber Company (The)

International Business Machines Corp.
International Paper Co.
McDonald's Corp.
Merck & Co.
Minnesota Mining & Manufacturing Co.
J.P. Morgan
Philip Morris Cos.
Procter & Gamble Co.
Sears Roebuck & Co.
Texaco
Union Carbide Corp.
United Technologies Corp.
Westinghouse Electric Corp.
F.W. Woolworth Co.

INDEX

abbreviations 10-11
  ampersands in 10
  definite article with 10
  formed of upper and lower case letters 10
  genitives of 10
  hyphens in 10
  list of 88-9
  lower case when written in full 11
  numerals in 10
  plurals 10
  roman type 10
  small capitals in 10, 63
  of titles of people 11
  to be spelt out 11
  two together 10
  use full form on first appearance 10
  very familiar 10
  which can be pronounced 10
accents
  foreign 89
  on French names and words 12
  on words accepted as English 12
accountancy ratios 90-1
acronyms, see abbreviations
active tense, prefer to passive 5, 12
acts of parliament, capitals for 16-17
acute accents 89
address, forms of 70
  abbreviated 11
adjectives
  formed from two or more words, use of
    hyphens 34
  from proper nouns 58
  hyphenated, in AmEng 79
  use for precision 71
adverbs
  position of in AmEng and BrEng 13, 75
  position in BrEng 12, 13
  used adjectivally with hyphens 34
aircraft names, italics for 38
aircraft type, hyphens in 30, 34
ambiguities, hyphens to avoid 34
American English
  and British English 73-86
  spelling 63
Americanisms, use in BrEng 13
ampersands 14
  in abbreviations 10
antithesis, use of colon 59
apostrophes 58
  with abbreviations 10
  after plurals 58
areas, capitals or lower case for 18
article
  definite, in abbreviations 10
  definite, in names of newspapers 38
  definite, with place names 49
  indefinite 14

Beaufort Scale 92-3
Bible, books of the 38
books, titles of
  punctuation 38
  in roman 38
brackets 58

  with abbreviations 10
  and position of commas 59
  see also square brackets
British English
  and American English 73-86
  spelling 63-7
brokers, singular form of verb with 21
buildings, capitals for 18

calendars 94-5
calibres, hyphens for 30
capitals 16-19
  in headings, etc 10
  small in abbreviations 10, 11
  for titles or ranks 16; see also lower case
captions, 10, 69
  roman in The Economist 38
cars, international vehicle registration letters 95-6
cedilla 12, 89
Chinese names 45
circumflex 89
circumlocutions, avoid 5
cities
  capital, avoid use as synonyms for governments
    49
  instances of use of lower case 18
  spellings listed 96-7
clauses
  commas round inserted 59
  hanging 33
clichés 20
collective nouns 20-1
  number of verb governed by 20
colons 58-9
commas 59
  in lists, AmEng compared with BrEng 85
commissions, lower case for ad hoc 17
committees, lower case for ad hoc 17
commodities, SITC descriptions 97-100
companies, public limited listed 138-40
company, singular form of verb with 20
company names 64
  ampersands in 14
  forms of 21-2
compass, hyphens for quarters of 35
compound words, AmEng 79
conditional sentences 41
constituencies, ampersands in 14
counties
  correct spellings of 133-8
  instances of use of lower case 18
countries
  choice of term of reference 23
  countries, singular form of verb with 20
cross-heads, ordinary capitals for 10
cross-references, in proof-reading 52
currencies
  list of countries and symbols 101-4
  lower case or capitals 24
  punctuation of abbreviated form 10
  typographical references for 24
currency, standard 24

dashes 59
  AmEng usage compared with BrEng 85

in dates 36
  with figures 30
dates
  dashes in 36
  hyphens in 36
  punctuation of 25, 59
  when referring to 14, 29, 36
decimals, prefer fractions 29
departments, capitals for 16-17
dictionary, AmEng and BrEng 76-7
diminutives, avoid 70
directional regions, upper or lower case 18
Dutch names 45

earthquakes 105
eg 10
elements
  capitals for 11
  isotopes of 11
  list of names and symbols 106-7
em-rule 85
en-rule 85
ethnic groups
  AmEng and BrEng 75-6
  references to 27-8
euphemisms, avoid 5, 27
exclusivity, AmEng and BrEng 74-5

family names, see surnames
figures, or number in words 29-30, 46
figures of speech 5; see also metaphors; similes
finance, capitals in references to 17-18
fonts, wrong 52
footnotes, italics in 38
foreign names 45
  capitals in composite 45
  problematical 48
foreign phrases, avoid 5
foreign titles, see titles of people, foreign
foreign words and phrases
  accents on 12, 37
  anglicised 37
  italics for 12, 37
  prefer Eng alternative 30-1
Fowler, F.G. 20
Fowler, H.W. 7, 20, 58, 59
fractions
  decimal equivalents 108
  hyphens in 29, 33
French names 45
French names and words, accents and cedillas 12
full stops 59
  in abbreviations, AmEng and BrEng 85
  with initials 37

genitives, of abbreviations 10
geographical areas, initial capitals 18
geographical assumptions 74
geographical names
  altered forms in historical references 18
  see also place names
geological eras 109
German names 45
German names and words, umlauts 12
government
  capitals in references to 17-18
  lower case 17

singular form of verb 20
government institutions, English form 63
Gowers, Sir Ernest 20, 59
grave accents 89
Gross, John 8

Hart's rules 60
Hazlitt, William 5
he/she 6, 62
headings
  no full stop at end 59
  omit titles of people 69
  ordinary capitals for 10
historical periods, upper case 19
historical references, altered forms of geographical
    names 18
hyphens 33-6
  in abbreviations 10
  absence of 35-6
  avoid overuse of 34
  in dates 36
  different AmEng and BrEng conventions 79
  with figures 30
  separating identical letters 35
  three words with 36
  to avoid ambiguities 34
  two-words with 36
  in word breaks 53
hypotheses, subjunctive in 6-7, 41

ie 10
imperatives, avoid 6
imperial measures 86
Indonesian names 45
infinitives, split 68
initials
  omit middle of people's names 70
  use of points 37
interest-groups
  assumptions about sex of 62
  circumlocutions promoted by 5
interpolations, in direct quotations 58
inverted commas, see quotation marks
italics 37-8
  foreign words in 12

Jane's "All The World's Aircraft" 30
jargon, avoid 5, 39
Johnson, Dr Samuel 23
journalese 63

Latin names, for animals, plants, etc 14
Latin words and phrases, with translations 110-12
laws, scientific, economic, facetious and fatalistic
    113-14
lawsuits, italics for versus or v 38
layout mistakes 52
lower case
  in abbreviations 10, 11
  miscellaneous uses 19
  for office holders 16
  for ranks or titles not followed by names 16

Malaysian titles of people 70
man words, alternatives to 62
manufactured goods, SITC descriptions 97-100
marginal marks, in proof-reading 53-7

measurements
American units compared with British 86
lower case for abbreviated forms 10
metric 115-17
national preferences 41
rough conversions 115-22
units with different equivalents 118-22
metaphors 5, 41-4
metric units 86
list of 115-17
prefixes 118
ministries, capitals for 16-17

national accounts, United Nations definitions 123
nationalities, precision in reference to 23, 62, 76
newspapers
definite articles in names of 38
italics for names of 38
nicknames, avoid 70
nouns
ending in -s but treated as singular 21
formed from prepositional verbs with hyphens 35
used as verbs 69, 74
see also collective nouns; proper nouns
number, use of verb with 20
numbers
in abbreviations 10
figures or words 29-30
numerals, Roman 132

office holders, lower case for 16
Olympic Games 124
opposition, lower case for 17
organisations
ad hoc in lower case 17
capitals for 16-17
definite article with abbreviated form 10
list with abbreviated titles 124-31
Orwell, George 5, 7, 41-2

pamphlets
punctuation of titles 38
titles in roman 38
paragraphs, length of 7
parenthesis, dashes for 59
participles, refer to subject 6
partnership, singular form of verb 20
passive tense, prefer active 5, 12
percentages 30, 48
periodicals, italics for names of 38
periods, see full stops
personal names
foreign, see foreign names
initials 48, 70
titles, see titles of people
see also surnames
Pinyin spelling 45
place names 49-50
change of name 49
definite article with 49
English form 49, 63-4
and names of peoples 49
spellings of common 49-50
places, capitals for definite geographical 18
plays
punctuation of titles 38
titles 38

plural, to avoid sexism 62
plurals
in abbreviations 10
spelling of certain 50-2
points, see full stops
political areas, initial capitals 18
political party
capitals for 17
singular form of verb 20
political terms, upper case 19
possessives, apostrophes in 58
prefixes 28
with hyphens 33-4
metric system 118
prepositions
after verbs, be sparing in use of 71
at end of sentences 52
with certain verbs and nouns 20, 22, 25, 37, 61
in dates 29, 36
position with "both" and "and" 15
problem words, AmEng and BrEng 75, 79-85
proof-reading 52-7
marks 53-7
proper nouns, adjectives from 58
provinces
correct spellings of 133-8
instances of use of lower case 18
punctuation 58-60
of abbreviated measurements 10
differences in AmEng and BrEng 85
placing with quotation marks 60, 85-6

quotation marks 60
and punctuation placing 60
AmEng compared with BrEng 85-6
for titles of books, pamphlets etc. 38
uses of single and double 60
AmEng compared with BrEng 85-6
quotations
broken off and resumed 60
interpolations in direct 58
use of colon before 58

race, AmEng and BrEng terms 75-6
radio programmes 38
ratios
accountancy 90-1
spell out "to" 29-30
regions
capitals or lower case for 18
correct spellings of 133-8
Richter scale for earthquakes 105
Roman numerals 132
rough descriptions, in lower case 17
rubrics
no full stop at end 59
in ordinary capitals 10

scientific units, named after individuals,
abbreviations 10-11
scientific words, avoid 5
semi-colons 60
sentence structure, AmEng and BrEng 75
sentences
conditional 41
ending in prepositions 52
keep short 59

never start with figures 29, 46
use simple 7
sex, or gender 32
sexism 62
AmEng and BrEng 75-6
ships 38
short words, prefer 5, 62-3
SI units 86, 115-17
similes 5
small capitals, for abbreviations 63
spacecraft names, italics for 38
special groups, ad hoc in lower case 17
spelling 63-7
AmEng and BrEng 75
common problems in BrEng 64-7
different AmEng and BrEng conventions 78-9
split infinitives 68
square brackets 58, 60
Standard International Trade Classification
(SITC) 97-100
states
correct spellings of 133-8
instances of use of lower case 18
stock market indices 138-40
subjunctive, use of the 6-7, 41
suffixes 68
AmEng -ize and BrEng -ise 76
British English 11-12, 27
-ise 64, 76
British English, plurals 50-2
different AmEng and BrEng conventions 78-9
surnames
and forenames 70
in headings or captions 69
order in foreign names 45
syntax, AmEng and BrEng 75

tables, ordinary capitals for 10
technical terms 39
television programmes 38
temperatures 10
tenses, perfect 13
that 72
tilde 89
time, give in figures 69
titles of people 69-70
of aristocracy 70
for the dead 70
first mention 69
foreign 70
hyphens in 34
misleading 69
serving as names 70
women 70
trade names, upper case 19
transitive verbs 20, 25, 33, 72
translation, lower case for rough of a foreign name
17
treasury bills 18
treasury bonds 18
treaties, capitals for 16-17
"typos" 52

umlauts 12, 89
upper case, *see* capitals

verbs, with collective nouns 20-1

vocabulary
AmEng and BrEng 74
differences between AmEng and BrEng 75

Wade-Giles system 45
women
married but known by maiden names 70
preferred titles 70
word breaks 52, 53
hyphens in 53
word order 46, 47
words, to avoid 71